PIANO•VOCAL•GUITAR

Billboard®

TOP COUNTRY SONGS OF THE 80'S

Photographs courtesy of The Country Music Foundation, Inc.

ISBN 0-7935-0948-3

HL® Hal Leonard Publishing Corporation
7777 West Bluemound Road P.O. Box 13819 Milwaukee, WI 53213

Billboard TOP COUNTR

Page	Song Title	Artist	Year	Chart Positi
10	Any Day Now	Ronnie Milsap	'82	
13	Are The Good Times Really Over For Good	Merle Haggard	'82	
16	As Long As I'm Rockin' With You	John Conlee	'84	
24	Baby's Got Her Blue Jeans On	Mel McDaniel	'85	
19	Chair, The	George Strait	'85	
28	Closer You Get, The	Alabama	'83	1
33	Coward Of The County	Kenny Rogers	'80	
44	Crying My Heart Out Over You	Ricky Skaggs	'82	
48	Diggin' Up Bones	Randy Travis	'86	
58	Do Ya'	K.T. Oslin	'87	
64	Don't Close Your Eyes	Keith Whitley	'88	
53	Don't You Ever Get Tired (Of Hurting Me)	Ronnie Milsap	'89	
68	Faking Love	T.G. Sheppard/Karen Brooks	'83	
71	Forever And Ever, Amen	Randy Travis	'87	
86	God Bless The U.S.A.	Lee Greenwood	'84	
78	Good Ole Boys	Waylon Jennings	'80	
82	Grandpa (Tell Me 'Bout The Good Old Days)	The Judds	'86	
96	He Stopped Loving Her Today	George Jones	'80	
98	Highway 40 Blues	Ricky Skaggs	'83	
100	Honor Bound	Earl Thomas Conley	'85	
91	I Can Tell By The Way You Dance	Vern Gosdin	'84	
104	I Feel Like Loving You Again	T.G. Sheppard	'81	
106	I.O.U.	Lee Greenwood	'83	
109	I Was Country When Country Wasn't Cool	Barbara Mandrell	'81	
112	I Wish You Could Have Turned My Head (And Left My Heart Alone)	Oak Ridge Boys	'82	2
115	I'll Still Be Loving You	Restless Heart	'87	

SONGS OF THE 80's

Page	Song Title	Artist	Year	Chart Position
120	I'm Gonna Hire A Wino To Decorate Our Home	David Frizzell	'82	1
124	I'm No Stranger To The Rain	Keith Whitley	'89	1
131	If Hollywood Don't Need You (Honey, I Still Do)	Don Williams	'83	1
134	Islands In The Stream	Kenny Rogers/Dolly Parton	'83	1
139	Life Turned Her That Way	Ricky Van Shelton	'88	1
144	Little Good News, A	Anne Murray	'83	1
147	Lookin' For Love	Johnny Lee	'80	1
152	My Baby's Got Good Timing	Dan Seals	'85	2
155	My Heroes Have Always Been Cowboys	Willie Nelson	'80	1
158	Nobody In His Right Mind Would've Left Her	George Strait	'86	1
162	On The Other Hand	Randy Travis	'86	1
165	Roll On Mississippi	Charley Pride	'81	7
170	Set 'Em Up Joe	Vern Gosdin	'88	1
174	(Smooth As) Tennessee Whiskey	Roseanne Cash	'83	2
182	Somebody Should Leave	Reba McEntire	'85	1
179	Swingin'	John Anderson	'83	1
194	Tennessee Flat Top Box	Roseanne Cash	'88	1
186	Timber I'm Falling In Love	Patty Loveless	'89	1
190	To All The Girls I've Loved Before	Julio Iglesias/Willie Nelson	'84	1
199	Wandering Eyes	Ronnie McDowell	'81	2
204	Way I Am, The	Merle Haggard	'80	2
207	What's Forever For	Michael Martin Murphey	'82	1
210	Who's Cheatin' Who	Charly McClain	'81	1
214	Why Not Me	The Judds	'84	1
217	You Don't Know Me	Mickey Gilley	'81	1
220	You're The Reason God Made Oklahoma	David Frizzell/Shelly West	'81	1

Country music roared into the 1980s astride a bucking mechanical bull; and — for a few months — it was a glorious ride. Here's how it happened. A magazine article about the denizens of Gilley's blue-collar nightclub near Houston caught the eye of Hollywood and was, in a relatively short time, transformed into the movie, *Urban Cowboy*. Because it starred John Travolta and Debra Winger, two of the film industry's hottest stars at the time, the movie received massive media attention, both before and following its release in mid-1980. Its impact was so great that thousands of American bars and discos were turned into mini-Gilley's. And millions of people who had never been anywhere close to Texas began wearing cowboy hats and trying to ride mechanical bulls like the ones featured in the movie.

Introduction

By Edward Morris

But there was more to the craze. The film also drew heavily on country music and country performers for its soundtrack. Among the country acts spotlighted were Mickey Gilley, for whom the nightclub had been named, Johnny Lee, Anne Murray, Charlie Daniels and Kenny Rogers, as well as pop singers Bonnie Raitt, Boz Scaggs and Jimmy Buffett. The Urban Cowboy craze, however, was short-lived and had little enduring influence on the sound of country music. It generated more light than heat. But the movie did inspire or highlight such memorable No. 1 songs as "Could I Have This Dance," "Stand By Me" and "Lookin' For Love."

A far more durable phenomenon during the '80s was a group that first called itself "Young Country," then "Wildcountry" and finally "Alabama." Alabama made its chart debut in 1979 with "I Wanna Come Over." But it was their next chart record in early 1980 that made the quartet an irresistible music force. The song was "My Home's In Alabama." Although it rose only to No. 17, it introduced a sound and a viewpoint that continues to define the group. For the next several years, every single Alabama released would go straight to No. 1, including "Tennessee River," "Mountain Music," "Close Enough To Perfect" and "The Closer You Get." Within a period of ten years, the group sold more than 50 million albums and was voted the Country Music Association's entertainer of the year and vocal group of the year three times each.

Anne Murray

Alabama

Willie Nelson

Johnny Lee

Randy Travis

At about the same time Alabama was getting its start as a national music force, so was Ricky Skaggs. And just as Alabama became the model for such later self-contained groups as Restless Heart, Sawyer Brown and Shenandoah, Skaggs became the driving force for what would in time be called "the new traditionalists." In addition to his solid eastern Kentucky bluegrass credentials, Skaggs was also an attentive student of the country music of the 1950s. He was able to weld bluegrass and country honky-tonk into a sound that partook of both but was like neither. The result was such hits as "Don't Cheat In Our Hometown," "I Don't Care," "Highway 40 Blues" and "Crying My Heart Out Over You." Skaggs' work paved the way for country music's acceptance of the likes of the Judds, Dwight Yoakam, Randy Travis, Ricky Van Shelton and Keith Whitley.

Ricky Skaggs

Like Skaggs and Whitley, Naomi and Wynonna Judd were from the fertile song fields of eastern Kentucky. Until they made their breakthrough in 1983, this alluring mother/daughter team sang mostly for their own amusement. Their voices were so agile and their ears so unerring that they were able to embroider their country music with bright threads of folk, gospel, jazz and bluegrass. Their legacy lives on in "Mama He's Crazy," "Why Not Me," "Grandpa (Tell Me 'Bout The Good Old Days)," "Love Is Alive" and in dozens of other hits.

Texan George Strait was also a trendsetter. A disciple of such Western Swing pioneers as Bob Wills and Hank Thompson, Strait relied on a larger-than-usual band to provide the energy and versatility for his songs. In manners and appearance, he was closer to the clean-living silver-screen cowboy than to the louder and lustier urban cowboy. In his long trail through the '80s, Strait made his mark with dozens of hits, among them "The Chair," "Nobody In His Right Mind Would've Left Her," "Ocean Front Property" and "Famous Last Words Of A Fool."

In the second half of the '80s, vibrant new voices began dominating the charts. Of these, none was quite as authentically rural as that of Randy Travis. Travis first hit the Billboard country charts in 1979 under his real name, Randy Traywick. It was not until 1985, though, that Randy Travis emerged with "On The Other Hand." His rich, resonant vocals also created standards with "Diggin' Up Bones," "Forever And Ever, Amen" and "1982." Dwight Yoakam and Ricky Van Shelton surfaced as Travis' traditionalist contemporaries. Both returned to the past for some of their best-known early hits. Yoakam scored with such oldies as "Honky Tonk Man" and "Always Late With Your Kisses," while Shelton refurbished numbers like "Life Turned Her That Way" and "Don't We All Have The Right." Patty Loveless, whose soulful, hard-driving voice conjured up images of Loretta Lynn and Connie Smith, also moved in new-traditionalist territory, evidenced by songs such as "If My Heart Had Windows" and "Timber I'm Falling In Love."

I Was Country When Country Wasn't Cool . . . *Barbara Mandrell*

Even though she had made some waves in the late '70s, Reba McEntire did not develop fully as an artist until well into the '80s. She had her first top ten hit, "(You Lift Me) Up To Heaven," in 1980 and her first No. 1, "Can't Even Get The Blues," two years later. By the mid-'80s, she was country music's most celebrated female vocalist, a stature achieved through such songs as "Somebody Should Leave," "How Blue" and "Whoever's In New England." In the late '80s, McEntire was given a run for her money by the brassy and bluesy K.T. Oslin. From near total obscurity, Oslin sprang to the top with her 1987 feminist chronicle, "80's Ladies." She followed this door-opener with equally direct and unsentimental numbers such as "Do Ya" and "Hold Me."

The '80s did not, of course, belong entirely to new acts. Some of the best songs came from veteran performers: Merle Haggard, for instance, with "Are The Good Times Really Over" and "The Way I Am"; George Jones, with his heartbreaking classic, "He Stopped Loving Her Today"; Kenny Rogers, with "Coward Of The County" and his duet with Dolly Parton, "Islands In The Stream"; Ronnie Milsap, with "Any Day Now" and "Don't You Ever Get Tired (Of Hurting Me)"; Charley Pride, with "Roll On Mississippi"; and Willie Nelson, with "My Heroes Have Always Been Cowboys" and his duet with Julio Iglesias, "To All The Girls I've Loved Before." Barbara Mandrell was a powerhouse at the start of the decade, having just terminated a highly rated music and comedy series on NBC-TV. She proved her appeal with songs as diverse as "The Best Of Strangers," "In Times Like These" and "I Was Country When Country Wasn't Cool." A near fatal car accident in 1984 derailed her recording career to a point from which it never recovered.

One of the hottest duets during the early part of the decade was David Frizzell and Shelly West. He was the younger brother of Lefty Frizzell and she the daughter of Grand Ole Opry star Dottie West. Their first single together, "You're The Reason God Made Oklahoma," soared to No. 1 and earned them all sorts of industry honors, including the CMA's vocal duo of the year prize for both 1981 and 1982. The two also sought solo careers, and Frizzell scored mightily in 1982 with "I'm Gonna Hire A Wino To Decorate Our Home." Neither singer, however, gained the stature separately that the two had achieved together.

John Schneider came to country music after having achieved TV stardom on *The Dukes Of Hazzard*. He wasted no time in proving that he was serious about his new career. His first effort, "It's Now Or Never," went to No. 4, and he followed it with a series of No. 1's including "I've Been Around Enough To Know," "Country Girls" and "What's A Memory Like You (Doing In A Love Like This)." Dan Seals also sought a home in country music following his pop accomplishments with England Dan & John Ford Coley. And he found one. He made the Top 10 with "God Must Be A Cowboy" and "My Baby's Got Good Timing," among others. "Meet Me In Montana," his 1985 duet with Marie Osmond, became his first No. 1 country hit, but he matched it later with "Bop," "Everything that Glitters (Is Not Gold)" and many more.

Reba McEntire

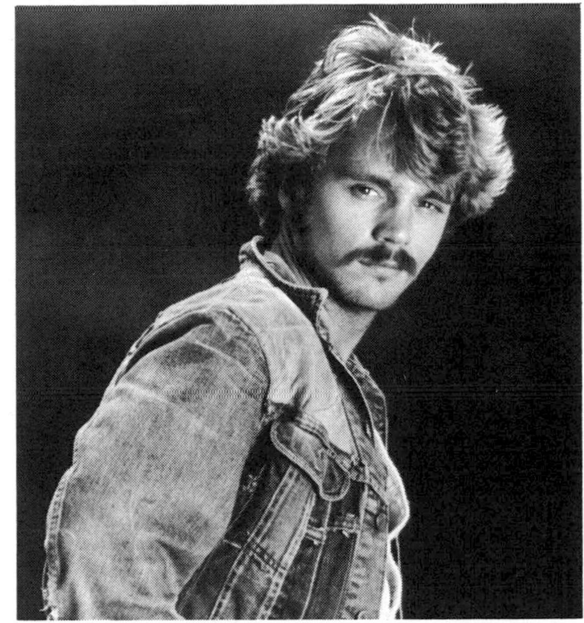

John Schneider

Lee Greenwood

Keith Whitley

God Bless The USA!
–Lee Greenwood

Among the unexpected hits of the '80s were John Anderson's madly infectious hymn to young ove, "Swingin'," and Lee Greenwood's intensely patriotic, "God Bless The U.S.A." The latter was a particular surprise, since it was released in 1984 during a period of relative calm.

Keith Whitley's story was the most tragic — and one of the most triumphant — of the '80s. After years of working to distance himself from his bluegrass roots, Whitley was finally, near the end of the decade, gaining recognition as a vocalist of extraordinary power and sensitivity. The song that demonstrated this talent beyond all argument was "Don't Close Your Eyes." Whitely turned out everal more major hits after this, including "I'm No Stranger To The Rain" and "When You Say Nothing At All." But it all tumbled to an end in 1989 when, at the age of 33, Whitley died of an alcohol overdose.

t seems certain that the 1980s will be looked back upon by historians as country music's Second Golden Age (the first being the 1950s). No other period produced as many first-rate singers, players, producers and songwriters as this one. Yet never has a musical period been truer to the best of its past.

ANY DAY NOW

Words and Music by BOB HILLIARD
and BURT BACHARACH

C11
F
F
lone,
down,
oh.
oh.
An-y
mp
Dm
Am
B♭maj7
A7+5
I know I should-n't want to
keep you
if you
don't
want to
stay.
And
mf
Dm
Am
Dm
Am
yet
un-til you're gone for-ev-er
I'll be
hold-ing
on
for dear
Dm
C11
life,
hold-ing you this
way,
beg-gin' you to
F
F6
Am
stay.
An-y
Day Now
when the clock strikes
go,
you'll call it
mp

Bbmaj7
Bdim
off, And then my tears will flow. Then my
mf
F
A7/C#
Dm
Gm7-5
wild beau - ti - ful bird you will have flown
blue shad - ows will fall all o - ver town,
oh. An - y
f
F/C
C11
Day Now love will let me down, cause you won't be a -
F
Gm7
Bdim
round. And the
F
Dm
round. An-y
mf
f
F/C
C11
F
Dm
Repeat and Fade
Day Now when you won't be a - round An-y

ARE THE GOOD TIMES REALLY OVER FOR GOOD

Words and Music by MERLE HAGGARD

G
D
G
yes- ter-day, when a man could still work, and still would,___ Is the best of___ the free life be-
ov -ens,___ when a girl could still cook, and still would,___ Is the best of___ the free life be-
A7
3
3
D
hind us now, and are the good times real-ly o - ver___ for good.___ Are we roll - in' down
hind us now, and are the good times real-ly o - ver___ for good.___ Stop roll - in' down
G
hill like a snow - ball head-ed___ for hell,
hill like a snow - ball head-ed___ for hell,
A
3
D
With no kind of chance___ for the flag or the lib -er - ty bell.___
Stand up for the flag,___ and let's all ring the lib - er - ty bell.___

I wish a Ford or a Che-vy would still last ten
Let's make a Ford and a Che-vy that'll still last ten
G
years like they should.
years like they should.
Is the best of the
The best of the
A7
free life be - hind us now,
free life is still yet to come,
And are the good times real-ly o - ver for
And the good times ain't o - ver for
D
A7
D
A7
1 D
A7
2 D
good.
good.
I wish

AS LONG AS I'M ROCKIN' WITH YOU

2
G
C6
D
I may nev - er have
C
G
C
much sil - ver and gold.
And
D
C
G
I've got some - thin' more pre - cious and warm - er to hold.
Em
And that old rock - in' chair don't scare me like it

Additional Verses:

3. Wherever I'm workin', whatever it's payin'
   It doesn't matter long as it's workin' with you
   Workin' with you.

4. These things I believe in some people call dreamin'
   It doesn't matter long as I'm dreamin' with you
   Dreamin' with you.

   (CHORUS)

THE CHAIR

Words and Music by HANK COCHRAN
and DEAN DILLON

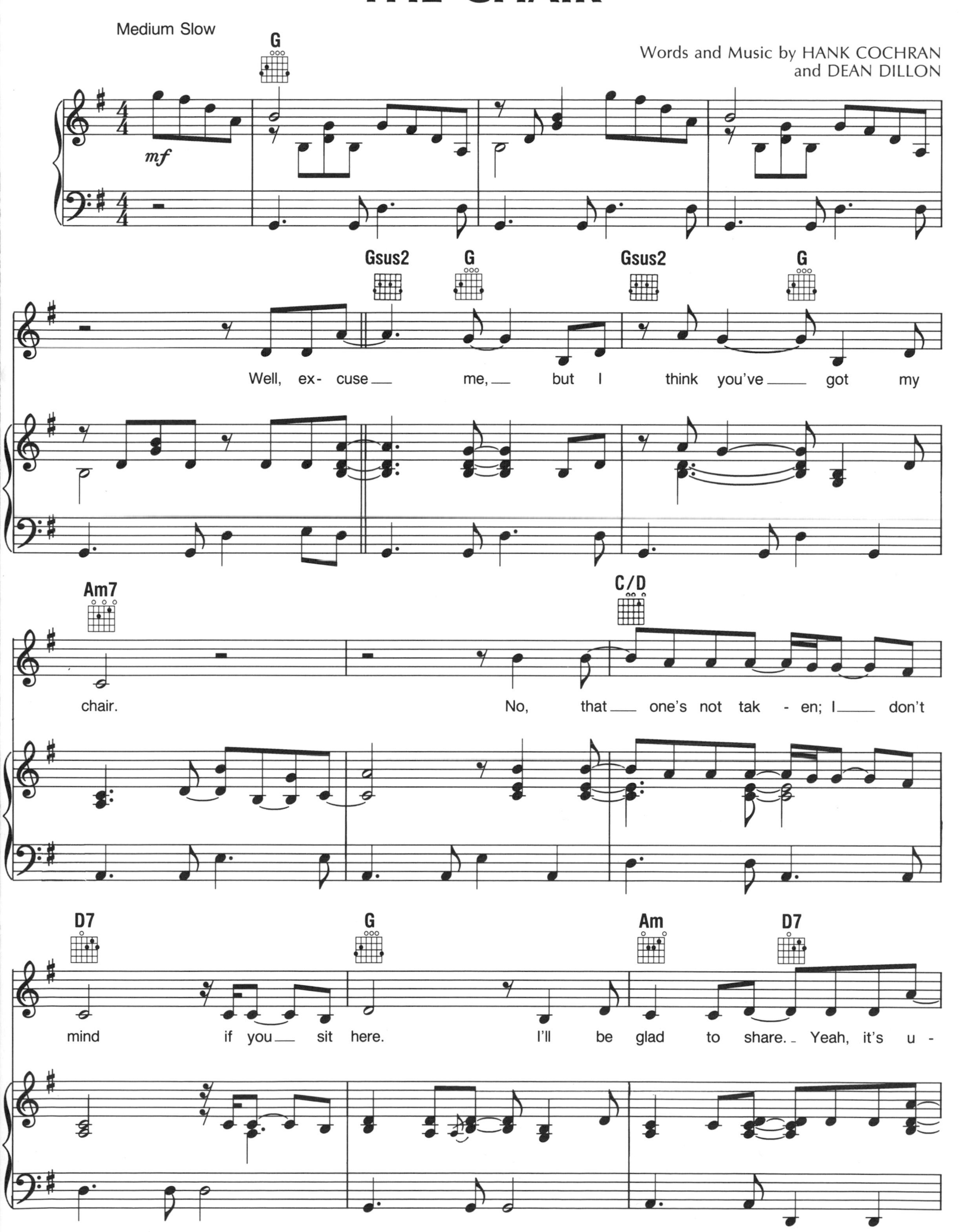
Medium Slow
G
mf
Gsus2
G
Gsus2
G
Well, ex- cuse me, but I think you've got my
Am7
C/D
chair. No, that one's not tak - en; I don't
D7
G
Am
D7
mind if you sit here. I'll be glad to share. Yeah, it's u -

Gsus2
G
Gsus
G
Am7
- sually packed here on Fri - day nights.
C/D
D7
Oh, if you don't mind, could I talk you out of a light.
G
Gsus2
G
Well, thank you, could I
Gsus2
G
Am
D7
drink you a buy?
Oh, lis - ten to me. What I mean

Am7
D7
G
is can I buy you a drink?
Any-y-thing you please.
Am
D7
Gsus2
G
Gsus
G
Oh, you're wel - come. Well, I don't think I caught your name.
Am
C
Bm
Are you wait - ing for some - one to meet
Am
E7/G♯
Am
D7
G
you here? Well, that makes two of us; glad you came.

Am7
C/D
No, I don't know the name of the band, but they're good aren't
G
Am7
they? Would you like to dance? Yeah, I like the song too, it re-minds
C/D
G
me of you and me, ba - by. Do you think there's a chance that
Am
D7
G
G/F♯
lat-er on I could drive you home? No, I don't mind at all.

Em
C
Bm
Am
E7/G#
Oh, I like you too, and to tell you the truth that
Am
D7
Gsus2
G
Am/G
G
was - n't my chair af - ter all.
Oh,
C
Bm
Am
E7/G#
Am
D7
I like you too, and to tell you the truth that was - n't my chair af - ter all.
Gsus2
G
Am/G
G
rit.

BABY'S GOT HER BLUE JEANS ON

By BOB McDILL

Bb Eb Bb Eb Bb Eb Bb Eb
Up by the bus stop and a-cross the street
Bb Eb Bb Eb Ab Eb
o-pen up their win-dows to take a peek, while she goes walk-in',
Ab Eb Bb Eb Bb Eb F
rock-ing like a roll-ing stone. Lord, have mer-cy! Ba-
Eb F7 Bb Eb Bb Gm F
-by's got her blue jeans on. She can't help it if she's

Eb Bb Eb Bb Eb F
made that way; She's not to blame if they look her way.
Gm F Eb Bb Eb F
She ain't real-ly try'n to cause a scene, it just comes nat-'ral - ly.
Guitar Tacet
Bb Eb Bb Eb
No, the girl can't help it.
Well, up on Main Street, by the tax - i stand,
Down on the cor - ner by the traf - fic light
Bb Eb Bb Eb Ab Eb
there's a crowd of peo - ple, and a traf - fic jam. She don't look back,
ev' - ry-bod - y's look - in' as she goes by. They turn their heads and they

Ab
Eb
Bb
Eb
Bb
Eb
she ain't do - in' noth - ing wrong.
watch her till she's gone.
F
Eb
F7
Bb
Eb
To Coda
Bb
D.S. al Coda
Lord have mer-cy! Ba - by's got her blue jeans on.
CODA
Bb
Eb
F
Eb
F7
Heav - en help us! Ba - by's got her blue jeans on.
Bb
Eb
Bb
Eb
Bb
Eb
Bb
Eb
Repeat and Fade

THE CLOSER YOU GET

Words and Music by JAMES PENNINGTON
and MARK GRAY

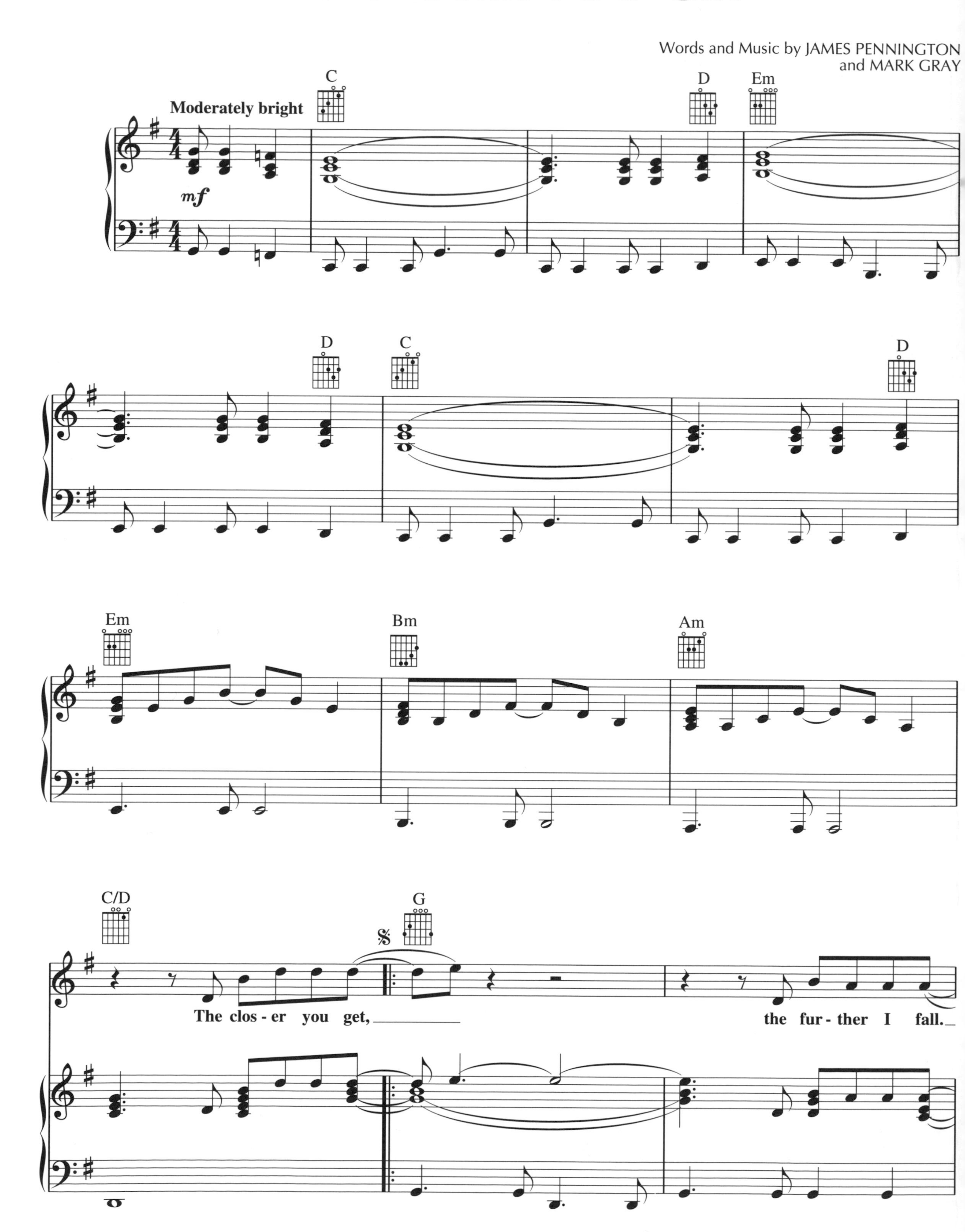

C
Am
I'll be o - ver the edge now
D
G
D
in no time at all.
I'm fall - ing fast -
G
C
- er and fast - er and fast - er with no time to stall.
Am
To Coda
C/D
The clos - er you get,
the fur - ther I fall.

G
F
C
The things that you say
Could I be dream-
D
Em
D
to me,
in'?
the look on your face,
Is this real-ly real?
C
D
Em
brings out the man in me.
'Cause there's some-thing mag - ic
Do I see a trace
the way that I feel
Bm
Am
1 C/D
in your eyes of love?
in your arms to-night.
The clos-er you get,

2
C/D
D.S. al Coda
The clos - er you get,
CODA
C/D
the fur - ther I fall,
C
D
C
keep fall - in', oh, yeah, yeah, keep fall -
D
C
D/C
- in', mm, fall - in', oh, yeah,
C
D/C
yeah, I'm fall - in'.

C
D/C
C
Yes, I'm fall - in'.
Yes, I'm fall - in'.
Yes, I'm fall - in'.
D/C
C
D/C
Yes, we're fall - in'.
Yes,we're fall -
Yes, we're fall - in'.
C
D
no chord
D.S. and Fade
- in'.
The clos - er you get,

COWARD OF THE COUNTY

Words and Music by ROGER BOWLING
and BILLY EDD WHEELER

Moderate Country 2
mf
C
F
C
Ev-'ry-one con-sid-ered him the cow-ard of the coun-ty,
He'd nev-er stood one sin-gle time to prove the coun-ty wrong.
G
C
His ma-ma named him Tom-my, the

F
C
folks just called him yel - low,
But some-thing al - ways
G
C
told me they were read - in' Tom - my wrong.
F
C
He was on - ly ten years old when his dad - dy died in pris - on,
I looked af - ter Tom - my 'cause he was my broth - er's son.

G
C
I still re - call the fin - al words my
F
C
broth - er said to Tom - my,
"Son, my life is o -
G
C
- ver, but yours is just be - gun.
F
C
Prom - is me son, not to do the things I've done,

F
C
G
Walk a - way from trou - ble if you can.
C
F
C
It won't mean you're weak if you turn the oth - er cheek, I
F
G
hope you're old e - nough to un - der - stand: Son,
G7
C
you don't have to fight to be a man." There's

Db
Gb
Db
some - one for ev - 'ry one__ and Tom-my's love__ was Beck-y,___
In her arms__ he did-n't have__ to prove he was a man._
Ab
Db
___ One day while he was work - in'___ the
Gb
Db
Gat-lin boys__ came call - in',
They took turns__ at Beck - y,__

Ab
Db
(Spoken) there was three of them!
(Sung) Tom-my o - pened up the door and
Gb
Db
saw his Beck - y cry - in',
The torn dress, the
Ab
shat-tered look was more than he could stand.
He
Db
Gb
Db
reached a - bove the fire - place and took down his dad-dy's pic - ture.

Ab
As his tears fell on his dad-dy's face, he heard these words a-gain:
Db
"Prom - ise me son, not to do
Gb
Db
Gb
Db
the things I've done, Walk a-way from trou-ble if you can.
Ab
Db
It won't mean you're weak if you turn

Gb
Db
Gb
the oth - er cheek, I hope you're old e - nough to un - der - stand:
Ab
Ab7
Son, you don't have to fight to be a man".
Db
D
The Gat-lin boys just laughed at him when he
G
D
walked in - to the bar - room. One of them got up and met him half-

A
D
- way 'cross the floor.___ When Tom-my turned_ a - round___ they said, "Hey
G
D
look! ol' yel-low's leav - in'." (Spoken) But you coulda heard a pin drop when
A
D
Tommy stopped and blocked the door. (Sung) Twen-ty years of crawl in'___ was
G
D
bot-tled up___ in - side him, He was-n't hold - in' noth-in' back___ he

A
D
let 'em have it all.
When Tom-my left the bar - room not a
G
D
Gat - lin boy was stand - in',
He said, "This one's for Beck - y." As he
A
D
watched the last one fall. (Spoken) And I heard him say, "I prom - ised you, Dad, not to do
G
D
G
D
the things you done, I walk a - way from trou - ble when I can.

A
D
Now please don't think I'm weak, I did-n't turn
G
D
G
A
the oth-er cheek, And Pop-pa, I sure hope you un-der-stand:
A7
D
Some-times you got-ta fight when you're a man."
G
Guitar Tacet
D
Ev-'ry-one con-sid-ered him the cow-ard of the coun-ty.
Slower

CRYING MY HEART OUT OVER YOU

Words and Music by CARL BUTLER,
MARIJOHN WILKIN, LOUISE CERTAIN
and GLADYS STACEY

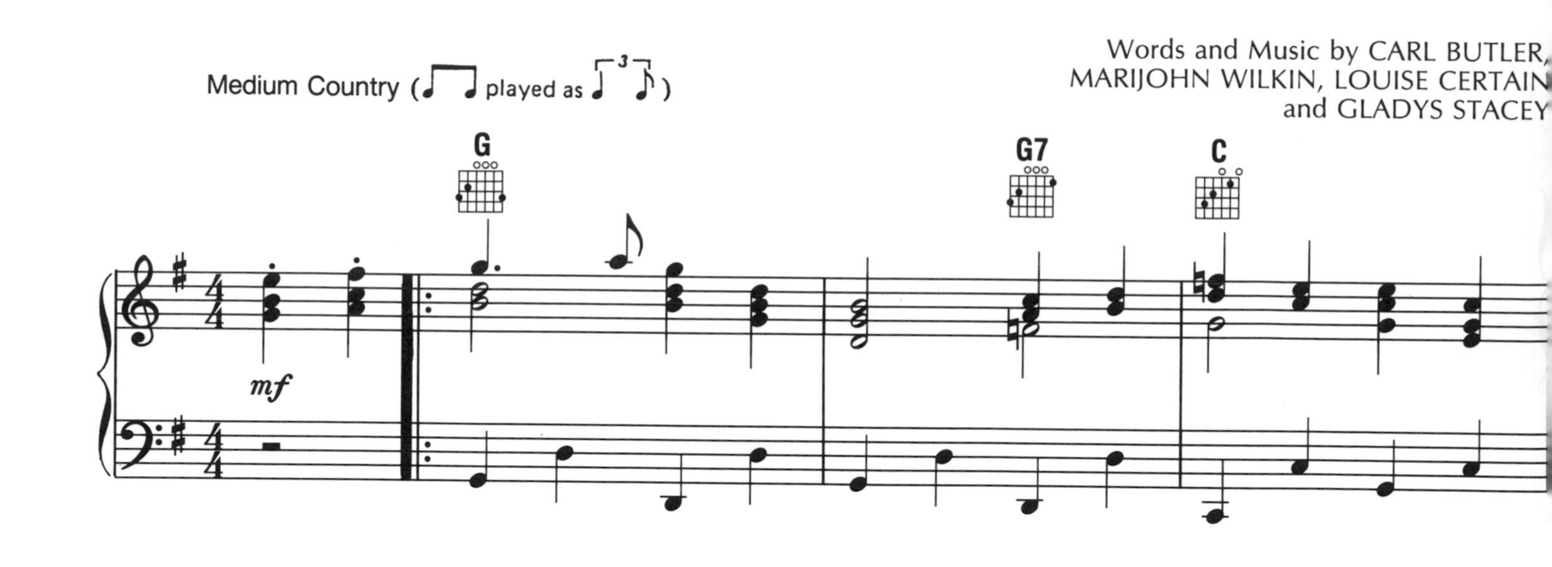
Medium Country (played as)
G
G7
C
mf

Am
D7
G

Off some - where the mu - sic's play - ing soft and low,
Each night I climb the stairs up to my room,

D7
and an - oth - er holds the
it seems I hear you
G
one that I love so.
whis - per in the gloom.
I was blind,
I miss your pic -
G7
C
I could not see that you meant the world to me,
- ture on the wall, and your foot - steps in the hall
D7
3
but like a fool I stood and watched you go.
while I'm cry - ing my heart out o - ver you.

G
Now I'm cry - ing my
heart out o - ver you.
D7
Those
Am
D
G
Gmaj7
blue eyes, now they smile at some - one new.
G6
G
Ev - er since you went a - way, I die a

C
D11
lit - tle more each day 'cause I'm cry - ing my
D7
1 G
heart out o - ver you.
2 G
Am
you.
D
G
Gmaj7
G

DIGGIN' UP BONES

Words and Music by NAT STUCKEY,
PAUL OVERSTREET and AL GORE

Moderate Country
mf

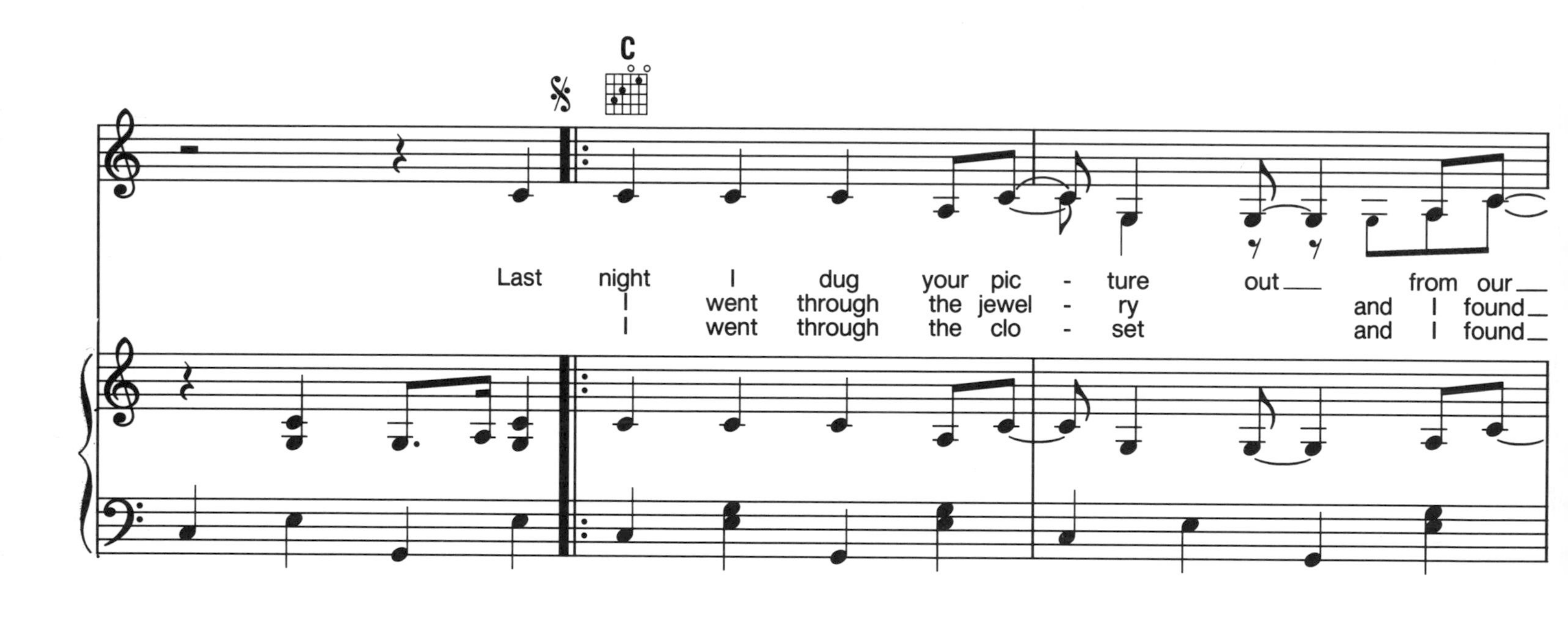
C
Last night I dug your pic - ture out from our
I went through the jewel - ry and I found
I went through the clo - set and I found

old dress - er drawer. I set it on the ta -
our wed - ding rings. I put mine on my fin -
some things in there, like that pret - ty

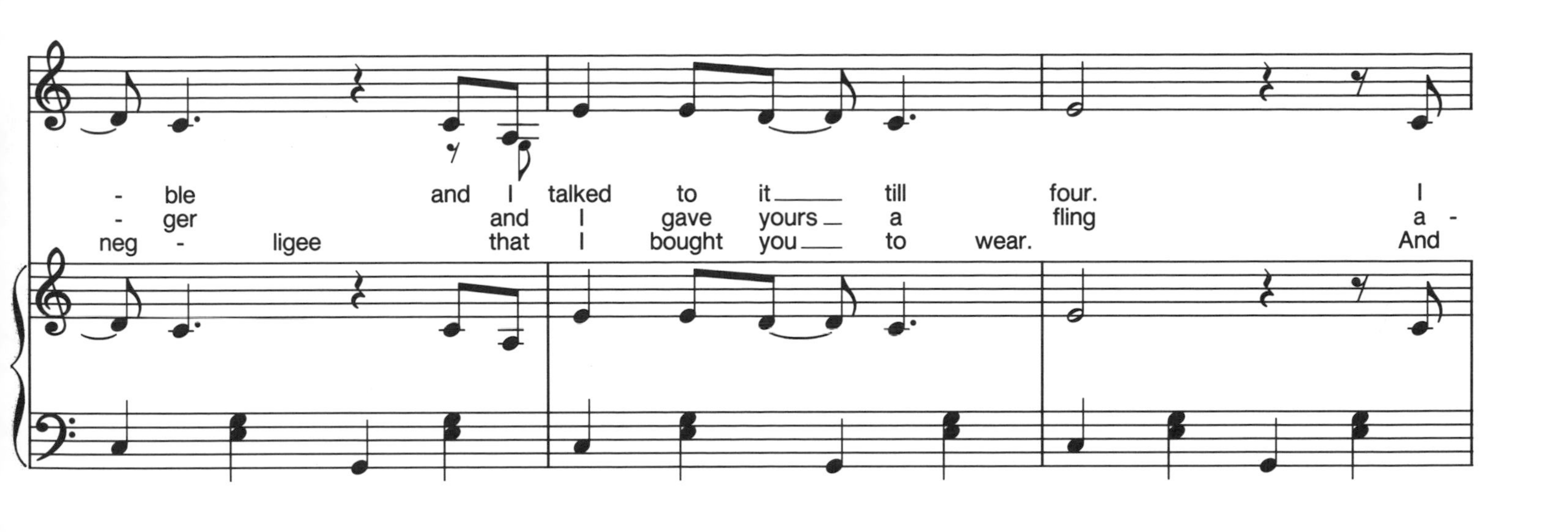
- ble and I talked to it till four. I
- ger and I gave yours a fling a -
neg - ligee that I bought you to wear. And

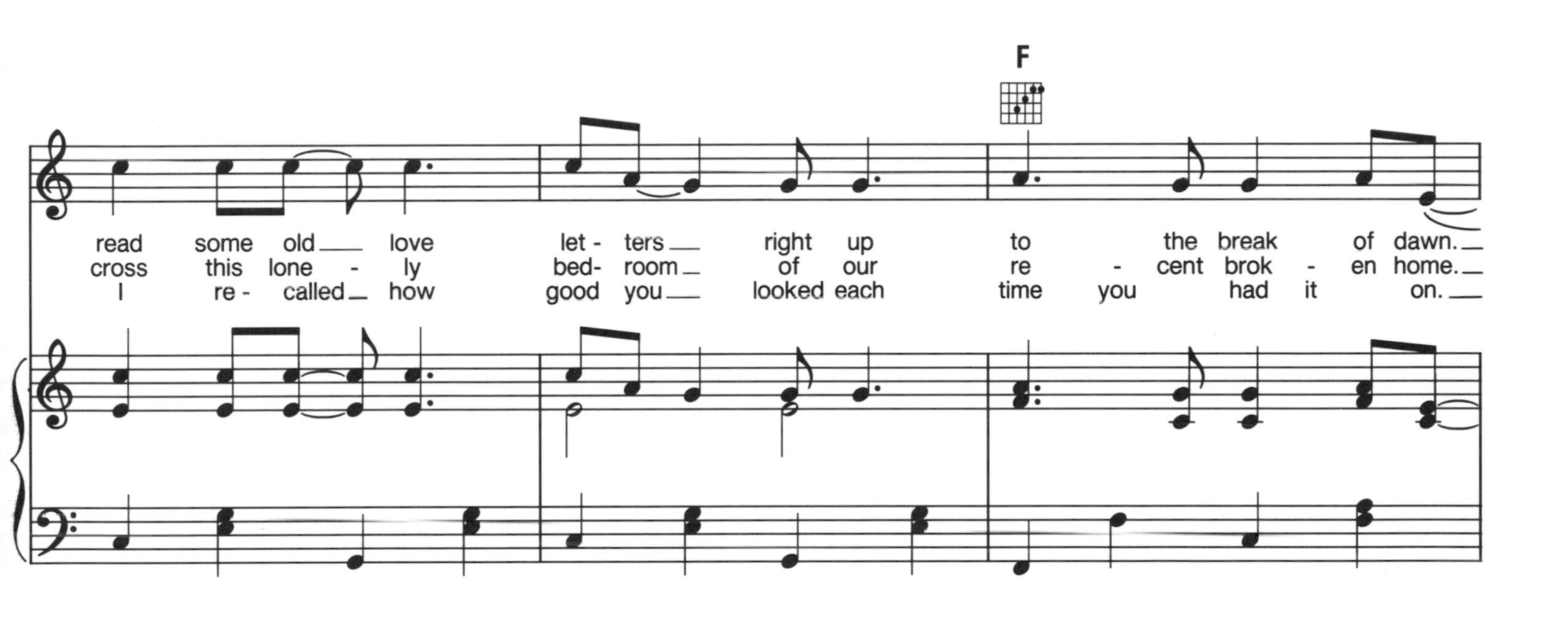
F
read some old love let - ters right up to the break of dawn.
cross this lone - ly bed- room of our re - cent brok - en home.
I re - called how good you looked each time you had it on.

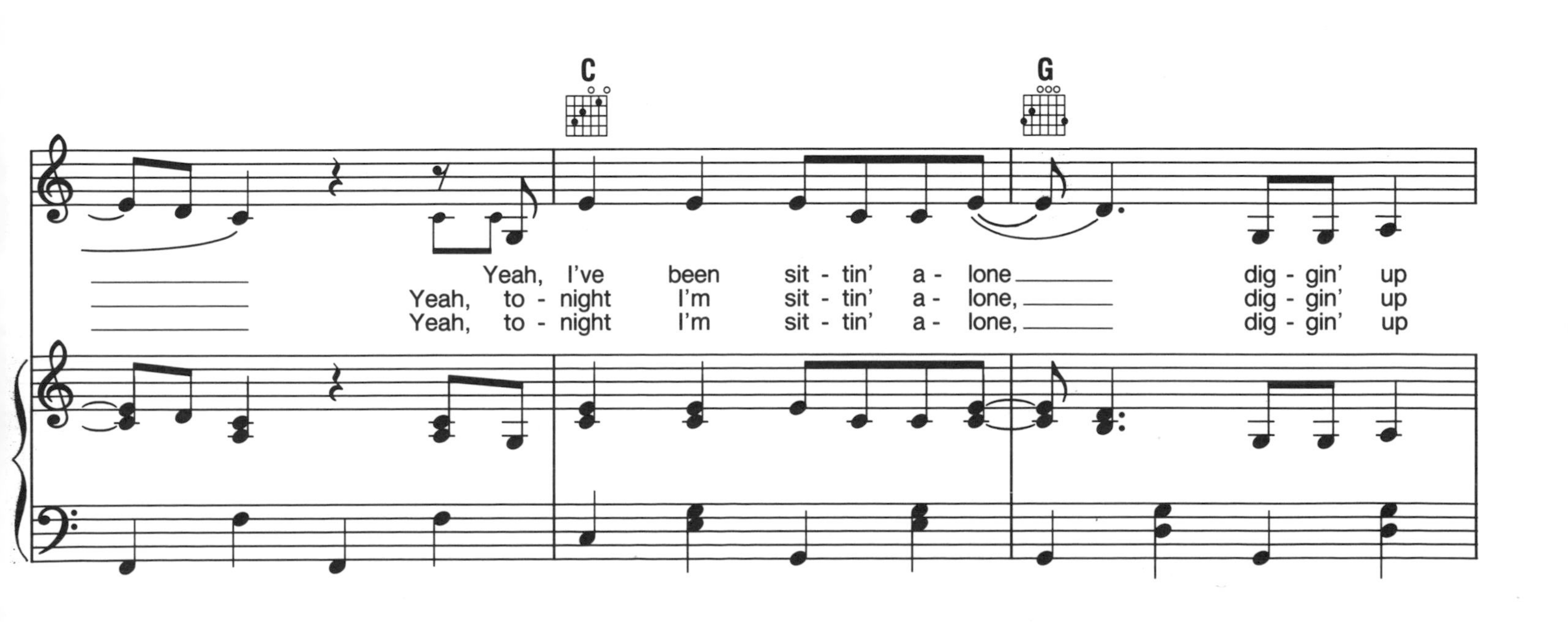
C
G
Yeah, I've been sit - tin' a - lone dig - gin' up
Yeah, to - night I'm sit - tin' a - lone, dig - gin' up
Yeah, to - night I'm sit - tin' a - lone, dig - gin' up

C
1
2,3
bones.
bones.
Then
I'm dig - gin' up
bones,
I'm dig - gin' up
bones,
Ex - hum - ing things that's bet - ter left a - lone.
C/A
G
Am
G7/B
C
And I'm res - ur - rect - ing

C/E
F
mem - 'ries of a love that's dead and gone. Yeah, to -
C
G7
To Coda
C
night I'm sit - tin' a - lone, dig - gin' up bones.
D.S. al Coda
And
CODA
C
bones.
bones,
instrumental
I'm dig - gin' up bones,

C/A
Ex - hum - ing things that's bet - ter left a - lone.
G
Am
G7/B
C
I'm res - sur - rect - ing
C/E
F
mem - 'ries of a love that's dead and gone. Yeah, to -
C
G
Repeat and Fade
night I'm sit - tin' a - lone dig - gin' up

DON'T YOU EVER GET TIRED
(OF HURTING ME)

Moderately (♪♪ played as ♩♪ triplet)

Words and Music by
HANK COCHRAN

F
mf

You make my eyes run

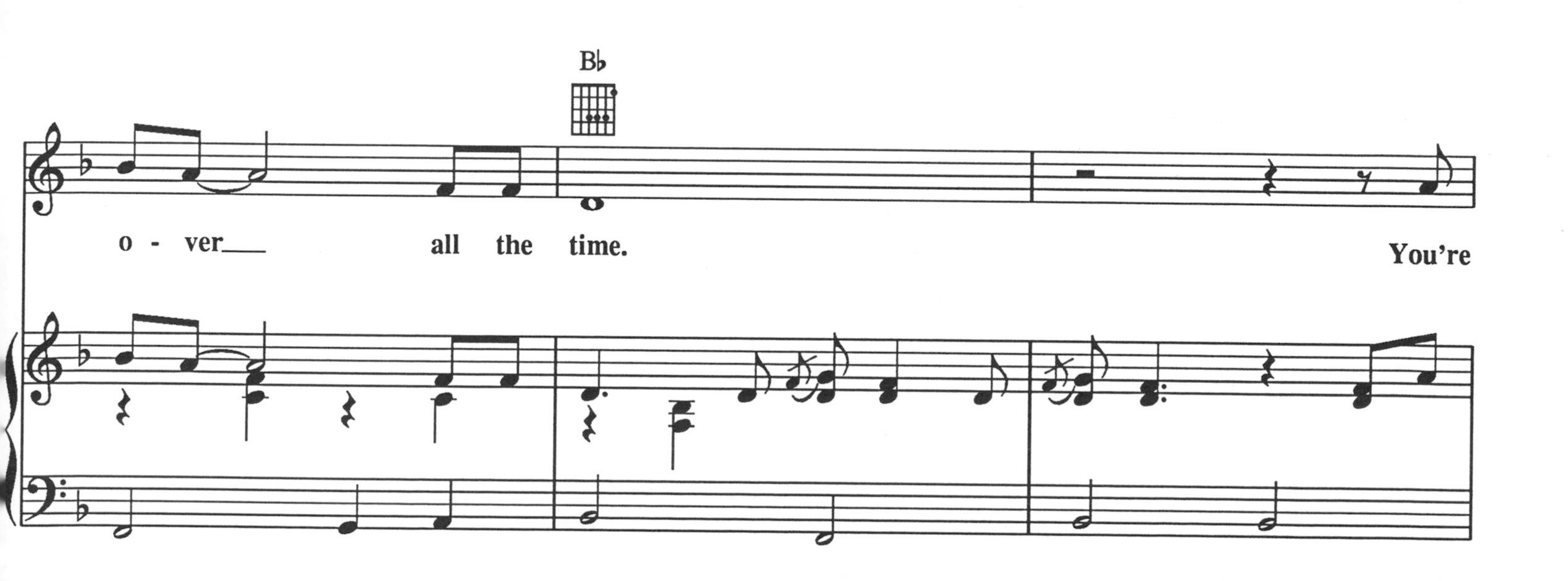
B♭
o - ver all the time. You're

C7
F
hap - py when I'm out of my mind.
you don't love me__ But you won't ___ let me
B♭
C
be. Don't you ev - er get
F
tired _ of hurt - ing me? You must

B♭
C
think I look bad with a
F
B♭
smile, For you have- n't let me
A+
A♭6
G7
wear one in such a long long
C
F
while. Still I keep com - in'

B♭
back.
How can this be?
C
Don't you ev - er get
F
tired of hurt - ing me?
To Coda
B♭

C7
F
D.S. al Coda
You must
CODA
C7
Don't you ev - er get tired of hurt - ing
F
Gm
F
me?

DO YA'

Words and Music by
K.T. OSLIN

Moderately slow, steady beat
G9
C/G
G
Am/G
mf
G
Do you still get a thrill when you see me
com - in' up the hill? Hon-ey, now do ya?
D
G/D
Do you whis - per my name just to

D7
G/D
D7
G
Am/D
bring a lit - tle com - fort to ya?
G
Do ya? Do ya still like the feel of my
G7
C
G/B
bod - y ly - in' next to
A7
D
ya? Well, I guess what I'm ask - in'

G
Am/G
To Coda
is do you still love me? do ya?
G
Oh, do you lie a-wake think-in' I'm the
D
G/D
big - gest mis-take you ev-er made?
Hon-ey, now
D
G/D
D
G/D
do ya?
And if just by snap-pin' your fin - gers you could

D7
G/D
D7
G
Am/G
G
snap them fin-gers and make it all go a - way,
hon-ey, now would ya?
Do you
G7
Am
G7/B
miss me when I'm gone but some - times
wish that I'd stay gone just a lit - tle bit
C
G/B
A7
D7
long - er?
Well, I guess what I'm ask - in'
G
Am/G
is do you still love me? Do ya?

G
C
'Cause, hon- ey, I sure do still love
G
you, least I think I do. and these
A7
ques - tions I'm ask - in' you could ask them of me
D
G/D
D7
D.S. al Coda
too. Lum de lum - de la do. Do you

CODA
G
D
Yes, I guess what I'm ask - in'
D7
G
Am/G
is do you still love me? Do ya?
G
G9
C/G
Do ya?
G
Am/G
G
Repeat and Fade
Oh, do ya? Well,

DON'T CLOSE YOUR EYES

Music and Lyric by
BOB McDILL

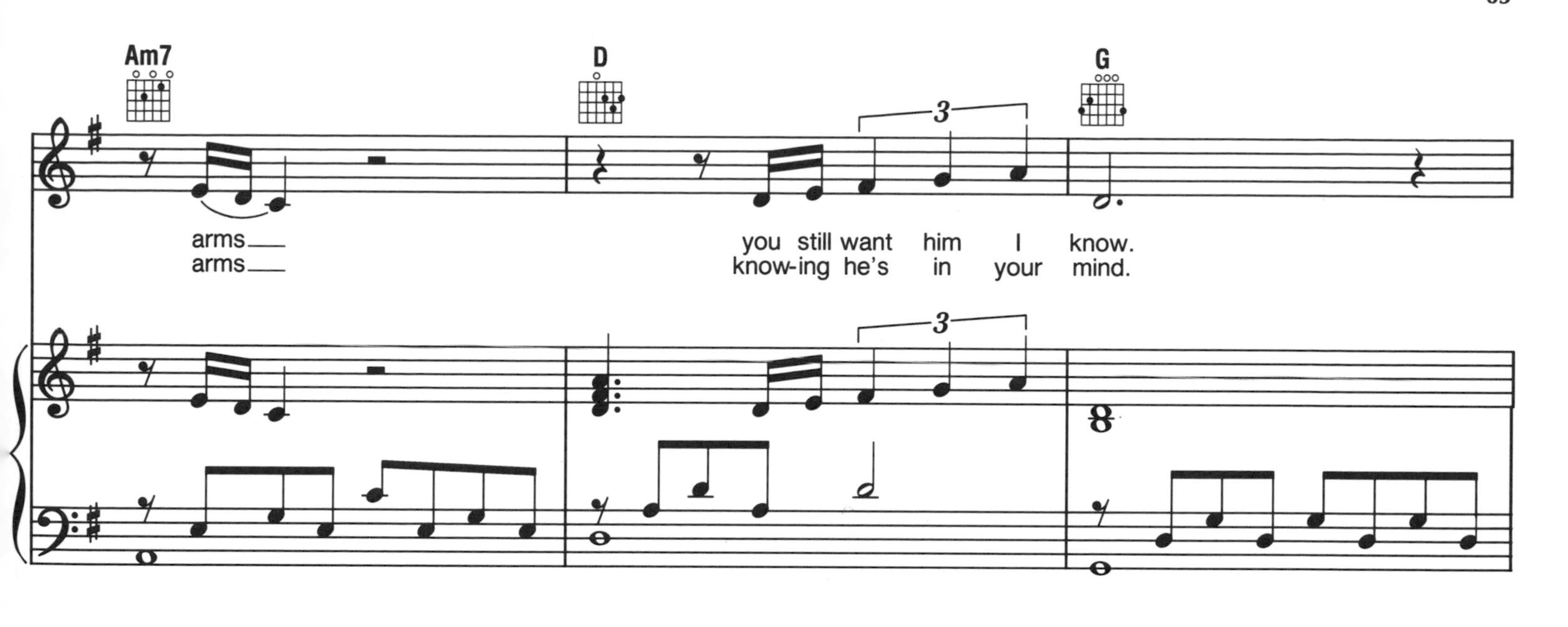
Am7
D
G
arms
you still want him I know.
arms
know-ing he's in your mind.

C
But, dar - ling, this time
But I keep hop - ing some - day

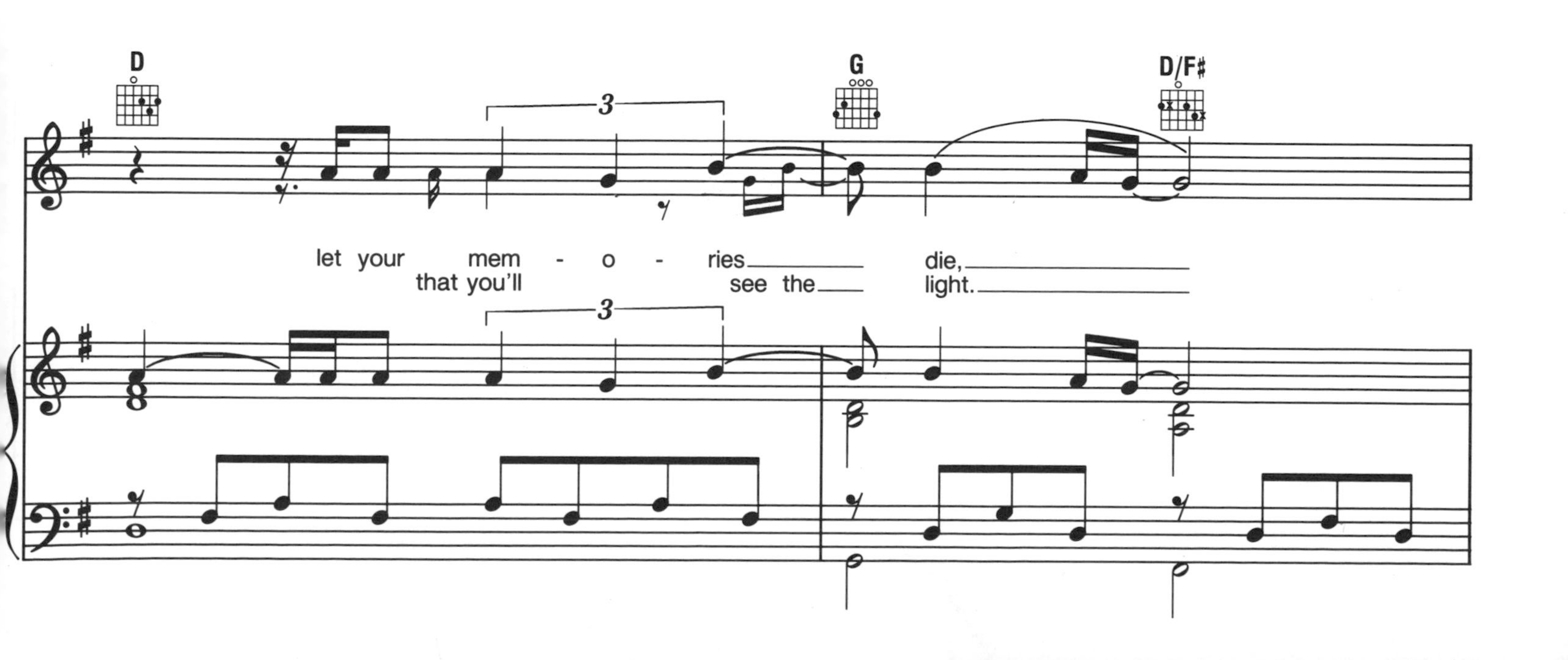
D
G
D/F#
let your mem - o - ries die,
that you'll see the light.

Em
C
When you hold me to - night
Let it be - gin to - night
D
G
C/G
G
don't close your eyes.
Don't close your
C
D
G
D/F♯
eyes. let it be me.
Don't pre-tend it's him
in some fan - ta -
Em
Am
D
sy.
Dar - ling, just once
let yes - ter - day go
and you'll find more

G
D/F#
Em
Am
love than you've ev - er known. Just hold me tight when you love me to -
D
C
G/B
Am7
G
night, and don't close your eyes.
C
G/B
Am7
G
Am7
eyes. Just hold me tight when you love me to -
D
C
G/B
Am7
G
night, and don't close your eyes.

FAKING LOVE

Words and Music by BOBBY BRADDOCK
and MATRACA BERG

Moderately Slow
mp

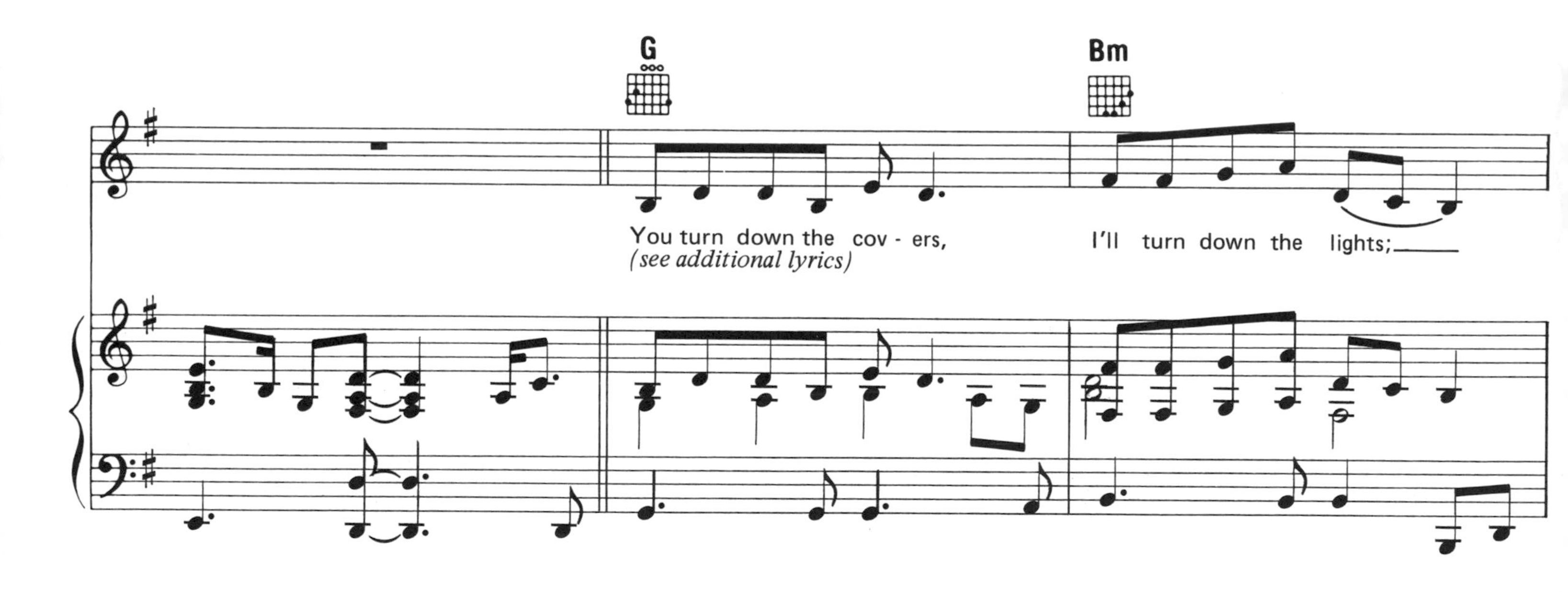
G
Bm
You turn down the cov - ers, I'll turn down the lights;
(see additional lyrics)

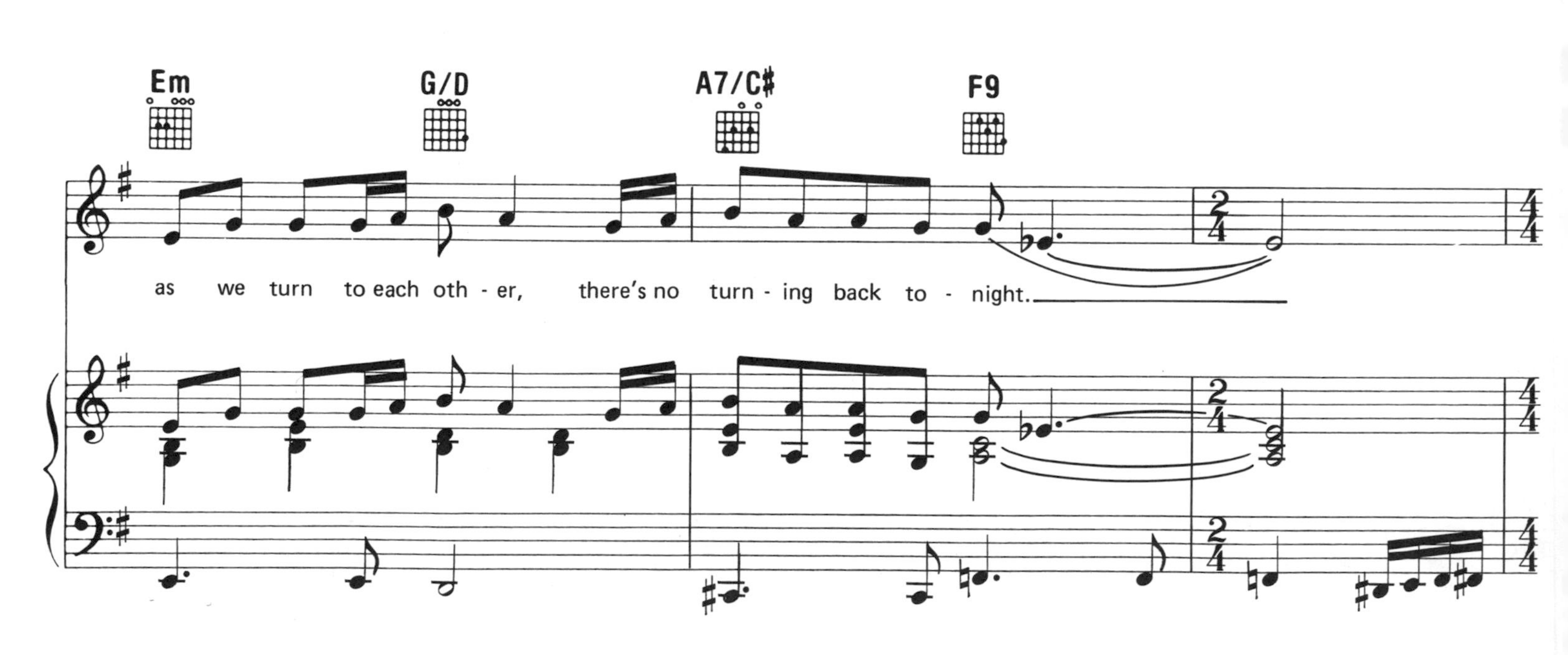
Em
G/D
A7/C♯
F9
as we turn to each oth - er, there's no turn - ing back to - night.

G
Bm
Em
C
I lay on "I love you," and you lay on your charms, as we lie here in each oth - er's
Bsus
B
Bm
D
Em
Bm
D
Em
arms fak - ing love, fak - ing love.
cresc.
f
Bm
D
Em
G/D
A7/C#
Am7/C
On - ly tem - po - rar - y lov - ers as we lie here to each oth - er.
Bsus
B
To Coda
1 Em
D
Em
2 Em
G6/D
We're just fak - ing love. love.
mf

You put on the coffee, I'll put on a smile;
We'll put each other on and laugh and talk a little while.
There's no use in crying for a feeling that's all gone.
We both knew we were lying all along.

FOREVER AND EVER, AMEN

Words and Music by DON SCHLITZ
and PAUL OVERSTREET

G
You may won - der how I can
Well, hon - ey, I don't care, I ain't in
D
E
pro - mise you now, this love that I feel
love with your hair, and if it all fell out
A7
for you al - ways will be. But
well, I'd love you an - y - way. They say
D
G
D
you're not just time that I'm kill - in'.
time can play tricks on a mem - 'ry,

G
I'm no long - er one of those guys.
Make peo - ple for - get things they knew.
D
G
As sure as I live
Well it's eas - y to see
D
this love that I give. is
it's hap - pen-in' to me. I've al -
E7
A
gon - na be yours un - til the day that I die.
read - y for - got - ten ev - 'ry wo - man but you.

D
G
Oh ba - by,
Oh dar - lin'
I'm gon - na love you for ev -
D
G
- er,
for - ev - er and ev -
D
- er, a - men.
As
G
D
long as old men
sit and talk a - bout the wea -

E7
- ther, as long as old wom - en sit and
A
D
talk a - bout old men; if you won - der how long
G
D
I'll be faith - ful
I'll be
well just
G
E7
hap - py to tell you a - gain.
lis - ten to how this song ends;

G
A
D
G
I'm gon - na love you for - ev - er and ev - er, for -
E7
A7
D
ev - er and ev - er, a - men.
1
G
A
D
G
E
A
D
They say

2
G
A
D
I'm gon - na love you for - ev - er and ev -
G
E7
A
- er for - ev - er and ev - er, for -
Bm
G
E7
ev - er and ev - er, for - ev - er and ev -
Asus
no chord
D
- er a - men.

GOOD OLE BOYS

Words and Music by J.L. WALLACE,
TERRY SKINNER and KEN BELL

Eb7
Bb
on the oth - er hand.
more than I could take.
you learn how to act.
You
And
How
Eb
Db
should-n't have led him on like that, it real - ly made me
when they helped him off the floor, he sure was look - in'
should I know where you left your damn ol' purse, hot dang you made me
Ab
Eb
mad. Us good ole boys will be good ole boys un - til their
sad. Oh, but us good ole boys will be good ole boys un - til their
mad. Ah good ole boys will be good ole boys un - til their
Db
Bb
Eb
1 Db
Bb
good ole girls go bad.
good ole girls go bad.
good ole girls go bad.
I

2,3
Db
Bb
Eb
Ab
CHORUS
Ab7
Yeah, good ole boys will be good ole boys until their
Well, good ole boys will be good ole boys until their
Eb
Eb7(#9)
Ab
good ole girls go wrong. I might even have
good ole girls go wrong. I might even have
Ab7
Bb7(#9)
Bb7
let him off if you hadn't led him on. Ah but
let him off if you hadn't led him on. Well I
Eb7
Eb
Db
you just kept on flirting, I guess I lost my
hope you learned your lesson and remember what I

Ab
Eb
To Coda
head. Ah but good ole boys will be good ole boys un-til their
said. Us good ole boys will be good ole boys un-til their
Db
Bb
Eb
D.S. al Coda
(3rd ending)
good ole girls go bad. Oh
CODA
Db
Bb
good ole girls go
Eb
Ab
Eb
D
Eb
bad.
(♮)

GRANDPA (TELL ME 'BOUT THE GOOD OLD DAYS)

Words and Music by
JAMIE O'HARA

A
D
zy.
Grand - pa,
And Grand - pa,
G
take me back to yes - ter- day
let's wan - der back in - to the past,
when the line be-tween
then paint me the
D
A7
D
right and wrong
pic - ture
did-n't seem so haz - y.
of long a - go.
G
Did lov - ers real - ly fall in love to stay,
and stand be - side each

D
A7
oth - er come what may. Was a prom - ise real - ly some - thing peo - ple kept,
not just some - thing they would say? (and then for - get) Did fam - 'lies real - ly
D
G
D
bow their heads to pray? Did dad - dies real - ly nev - er go a - way?
Em
G/A
Oh, oh, grand - pa, tell me 'bout the good old days.

1.
D
2.
D
Oh, oh,
Em
G/A
D
grand - pa, tell me 'bout the good old days.
G
D
A7
D
D.S. and Fade
Did fam - 'lies real - ly

GOD BLESS THE U.S.A.

F
Am7
thank my luck - y stars to be liv - in' here to - day, 'cause the
Gm7
Dm
Bb
flag still stands for free - dom and they can't take that a - way.
And I'm
Chorus
C/E
Bb/D
F
proud to be an A - mer - i - can where at least I know I'm free. And I
C/E
Bb/D
F
won't for - get the men who died, who gave that right to me. And I'd glad - ly

Dm
F/A
B♭
Am7
stand up; next to you and de - fend her still to - day. 'Cause there
Gm7
F/A
B♭
Gm7/C
ain't no doubt I love this land God bless the U S
F
Am7
B♭/F
F
B♭/F
A
(2.) From the
Verse
F
B♭/F
lakes of Min - ne - so - ta, to the hills of Ten - nes - see, a -

Gm7
Eb7
C7
cross the plains of Tex - as, from sea to shin - ing sea, From
F
Am7
De - troit down to Hous - ton and New York to L A Well, there's
Gm7
Dm
Bb
D. S. al Coda
pride in ev - 'ry A-mer - i - can heart, and it's time to stand and say That I'm
Coda
F
Bb
Gm7/C
Dm
Bb
God bless the U S A And I'm

Chorus
C/E
Bb/D
F
proud to be an A-mer-i-can where at least I know I'm free, and I
won't for-get the men who died, who gave that right to me. And I'd glad-ly
Dm
F/A
Bb
Am7
stand up next to you, and de-fend her still to-day. 'Cause there
Gm7
Gm7
Am7
C7
ain't no doubt I love this land God bless the U S A

I CAN TELL BY THE WAY YOU DANCE

Words and Music by ROB STRANDLUND
and SANDY PINKARD

E
A
B
words made me un - der - stand what's on your mind.
E
A
B
The rhy - thm of your bod - y close to
C#m
B
E
mine. I can tell by the way you dance
A
B
E
that you're gon - na love me to - night.

A
B
C♯m
B
E
A
D
Some-times it's cold.
Some-times it's hot.
A
B
E
B/D♯
Love's eith - er right or it's wrong.
C♯m
B
E
A
D
Feels so good, love you a lot.
A
B
Right here be-side me is where you be - long.

E
A
B
I ___ don't care if ev - 'ry-bod - y knows the way I
E
A
B
feel un - til the dream _ of hold - ing you is
C#m
B
To Coda
E
real. ___ I can tell by ___ the way ___ you dance ___
A
B
E
that you're gon - na love _ me to - night. ___

A
B
E
A
B
E
A
B
C♯m
B
E
A
B
D.S. al Coda
CODA
E
tell by the way you dance
A
B
E
A
B
Repeat and Fade
that you're gon - na love me to - night.
I can

HE STOPPED LOVING HER TODAY

Words and Music by BOBBY BRADDOCK
and CURLY PUTMAN

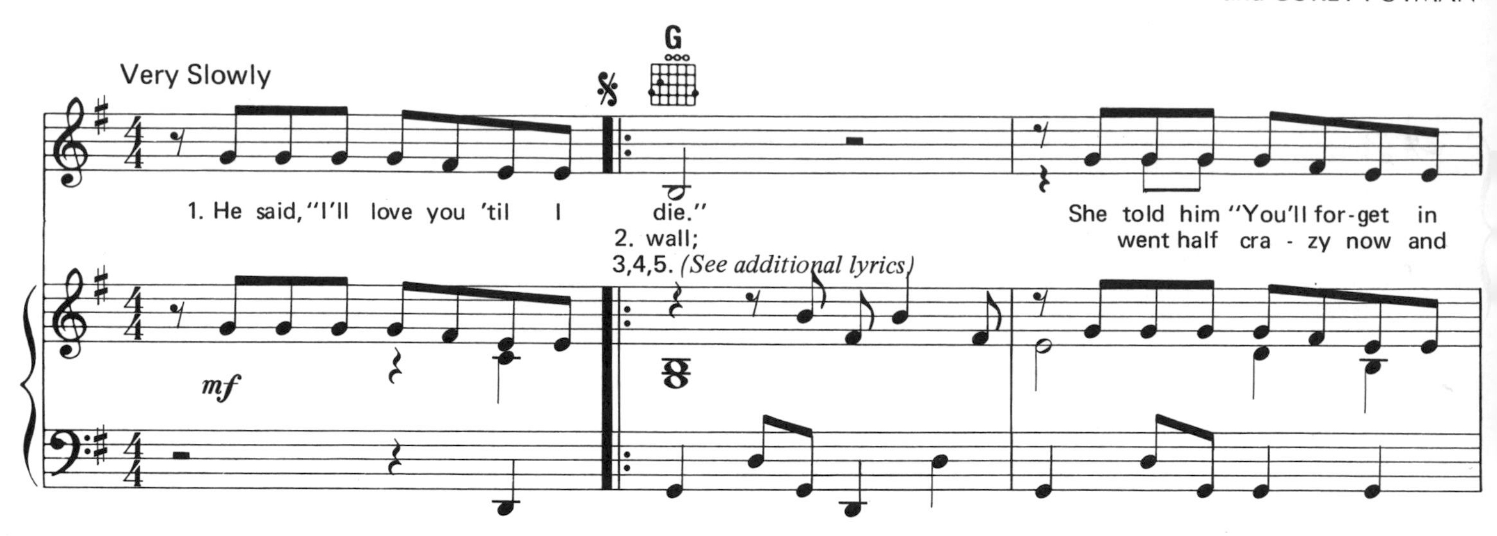
Very Slowly
G
1. He said, "I'll love you 'til I die."
2. wall;
3,4,5. (See additional lyrics)
She told him "You'll for-get in
went half cra - zy now and
mf

Am
D7
time."
then,
As the years went slow - ly by
but he still loved her through it all,

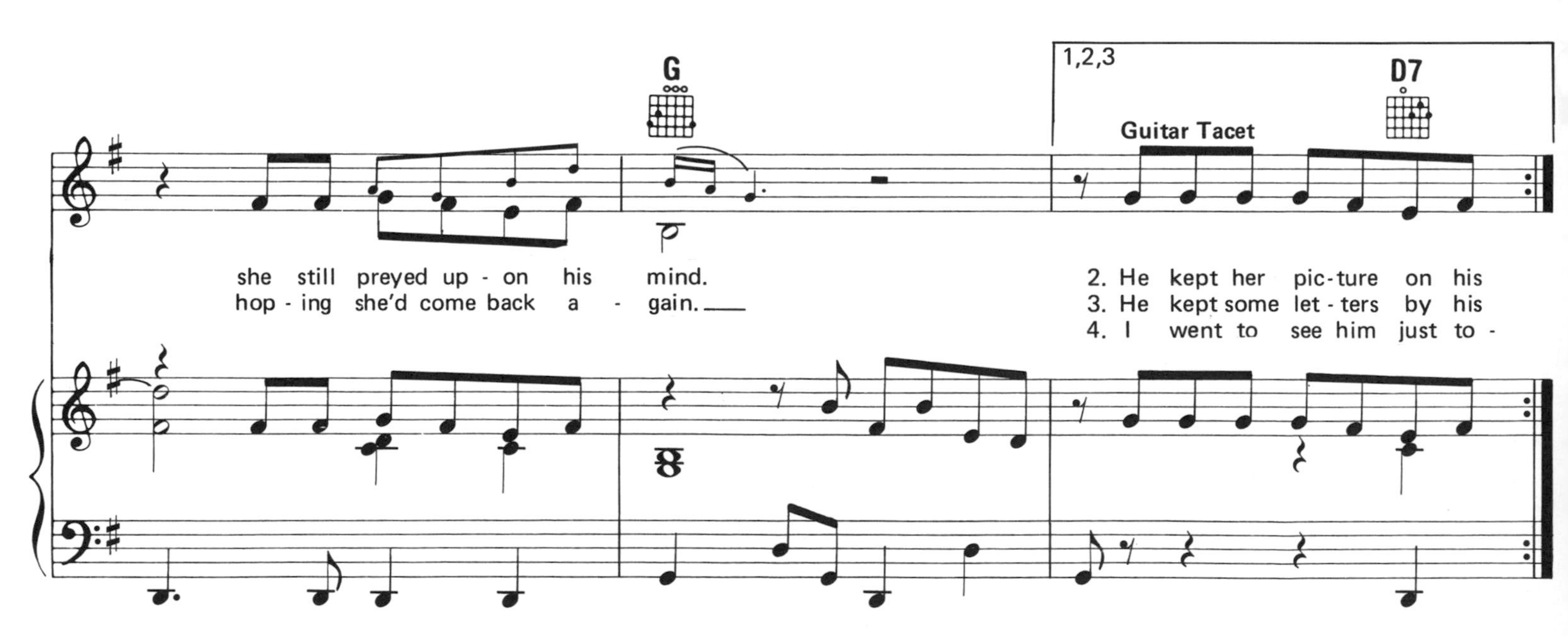
G
1,2,3
Guitar Tacet
D7
she still preyed up - on his mind.
hop - ing she'd come back a - gain.
2. He kept her pic-ture on his
3. He kept some let - ters by his
4. I went to see him just to -

Verse 3:
He kept some letters by his bed, dated 1962.
He had underlined in red every single, "I love you".

Verse 4:
I went to see him just today, oh, but I didn't see no tears;
All dressed up to go away, first time I'd seen him smile in years.
(To Chorus:)

Verse 5: *(Spoken)*
You know, she came to see him one last time.
We all wondered if she would.
And it came running through my mind,
This time he's over her for good. (To Chorus:)

HIGHWAY 40 BLUES

Words and Music by
LARRY CORDLE

A
B
Wast - ed time and mon - ey too, Squan - dered youth in search of
Shat - tered dreams my mind is numb, My mon - ey's gone stick out my
Well I've played the mus - ic halls and bars, Had fan - cy clothes and big fine
E
B
C#m
F#
truth, But in the end I had to lose. Lord a - bove I paid my
thumb, My eyes are filled with bit - ter tears. Lord I ain't been home in
cars, Things a coun - try boy can't use Dix - ie Land I sure miss
B
1,2 E
G
A
3 E
G
A
E
dues got the
years got the high - way for - ty blues.
you got the
blues.
F#m
B
E
G
D
A
E

HONOR BOUND

Words and Music by TOMMY ROCCO, CHARLIE BLACK and AUSTIN ROBERTS

Slowly (𝅗𝅥 = 1 beat)
L.H.
p
Bb
Eb/Bb
Bb
Noth-in's been said, noth-in's been done,
She's try-in' so hard, but it's tak-in' its toll.
Eb
Bb
It's hard to see a dif-ference be-tween the ris-ing and the set-ting
Try-in' to keep her heart warm with a love slow-ly grow-ing
F
Bb
Eb/Bb
sun. But I can feel a change, it's there in her
cold. Well, who knows what is right when ev-'ry-thing's

Bb
Eb
Bb
touch, It's sub-tle but it's deep and it hurts us both so
wrong. No mat-ter what I do now, it won't mat-ter when she's
F
Cm
Cm/F
much: Me, be-cause I'm los-ing her, and her be-cause she feels
gone; But how long can I keep hold-ing her, when she's on-ly hold-ing me.
Eb
She's hon-or bound
f
F7
Eb
Bound by a prom-ise that she made so long a-go; But I

F7
Eb
love her so much that I can't let her know I know. Oh, I
Cm7
Dm7
Eb
F
Gm7
Cm
Bb/D
know her pure heart made the prom-ise hon - est-ly; Oh, but how long can her
Eb
Eb/F
Bbsus
Bb
hon-or keep her bound to me.
1 Bbsus
Bb
2 Bbsus
Bb
Eb
Bbsus
Bb

Eb
F
Bbsus
Bb
Bbsus
Bb
Eb/Bb
Noth-in's been said,
noth-in's been done.
Bb
Eb
It's hard to see a dif - ference be-tween the
Bb
F
Bb
ris - ing and the set - ting sun.
p
ritard. e dim.
pp

I FEEL LIKE LOVING YOU AGAIN

Words and Music by SONNY THROCKMORTON
and BOBBY BRADDOCK

G
A
D
Dmaj7
D7
I feel like lov-in' you a - gain.
I should be o - ver you, but I'm not sure I am.
A7
Bm
D/A
If an-y-one can turn my world a - round, you know you can.
I feel like lov - in';
I feel like lov - in';
I feel like lov - in' you a - gain.

I.O.U.

Words and Music by AUSTIN ROBERTS
and KERRY CHATER

Moderately Slow Ballad

mf

G
Em
You be - lieve that I've changed your life _ for - ev - er _ and you're
- mazed when you say its me _ you live _ for _ and you

Am7
D7sus
G
D7
nev - er gon - na find _ an - oth - er some - bod - y like me. _ And you
know that when _ I'm hold - ing, you you're right where you be - long. _ And my

G
Em
wish you had more than just a life time to
love I can't help but smile with won - der when you
Am7
D7sus
give back all I've giv - en you and that's what you be - lieve. But I. O.
tell me what I've done for you, 'cause I've known all a - long that I. O.
G
D
C
Am7
D
Dsus
U. the sun - light in the morn - ing and the
G
Em
Am7
D
Dsus
nights of hon - est lov - in' that time can't take a - way. And I. O.

G
D7
C
Am7
D
U.
more than life, now more than ev - er.
I
G
Em
To Coda
Am7
D7sus
know that it's the sweet - est debt I'll ev - er have to pay.
1.
G
Gmaj7
C
D7sus
D11
I'm a-
2.
G
D7sus
D.S. al Coda
And I. O.
CODA
Am7
D7sus
G
Gmaj7
C
D
G
ev - er have to pay
rit.
a tempo
rit.

I WAS COUNTRY WHEN COUNTRY WASN'T COOL

Words and Music by KYE FLEMING
and DENNIS MORGAN

G/F
C
E
Am
C/G
F
all of my friends were dig-ging rock and roll, and rhy-thm and blues. I was
Dm
Dm7/G
Cmaj7
C6
C
1
Cmaj7
C6
C
coun-try, when coun-try was-n't cool.
2. I re-mem-ber
2,3
Cmaj7
C6
C
G
G6
G
G6
G
C
C6
C
Ooh, I was coun-try, when coun-try was-n't cool;
C6
C
G
G6
G
G6
G
C
C6
C
I was coun-try from my hat down to my boots.

Verse 2:
I remember circling the drive-in,
Pulling up, and turning down George Jones.
I remember when no one was looking,
I was putting peanuts in my coke.
I took a lot of kidding, 'cause I never did fit in;
Now look at everybody trying to be what I was then;
I was country, when country wasn't cool.

Verse 3:
They called us country bumpkins for sticking to our roots;
I'm just glad we're in a country where we're all free to choose;
I was country, when country wasn't cool.

I WISH YOU COULD HAVE TURNED MY HEAD
(And Left My Heart Alone)

Words and Music by SONNY THROCKMORTON

Bb
shake that thing and you know I'm not that strong, But I
C7
wish you could have turned my head and left my heart a -
1 F
- lone. Oh and I
2 F
lone.
Bb
First time I laid eyes on you, got caught up in your sway;

C7
Thought I did - n't have a chance and
Bb
F
then you looked my way. From the long - in' to the lov -
Bb
C7
in', girl, we've made it all the way, But for all the hun - ger in
C6
C7
Bb
F/A
Gm7
F
D.S. and Fade
Guitar Tacet
my eyes my heart has had to pay. Oh and I

I'LL STILL BE LOVING YOU

Words and Music by TODD CERNEY, PAM ROSE, MARYANN KENNEDY and PAT BUNCH

C(add9)
G/B
C(add9)
me
and I'll need you
for a life - time
C
Em
D
till all the moun - tains are val - leys,
un - til the last moon is ris - ing
Am7
C
D
and eve - ry o - cean is dry,
you'll see the love in my eyes,
my love.
my love.
E
A
I'll be yours un - til the
f

F♯m7
C♯m7
sun does - n't shine,
till time
stands still,
C
G
A
un - til the winds don't blow.
When to - day is just a
F♯m7
C♯m7
mem - 'ry to me,
I know
C
G
C
G
I'll still be lov - in',
I'll still be
lov - in' you.
lov - in' you.

D
To Coda
1
I'll still be
C
lov - in' you.
2
E
F♯/A♯
Amaj7
B
E
F♯/A♯

G#m
G
D
E
D.S. al Coda
CODA
C
I'll still be lov - in'_ you.
D
I'll still be lov - in',
I'll still be lov - in' you._
C
Repeat and Fade
I'll still be lov - in' you._

I'M GONNA HIRE A WINO TO DECORATE OUR HOME

Words and Music by
DeWAYNE BLACKWELL

G C F
you won't need to roam We'll take out the din - ing room ta - ble put a bar a - long that
favor-ite kind of beer And for you I'll al - ways keep in stock those soft a - lu-min-um
I won't cook no more There'll be Mon - day night foot - ball on T. V. a - bove the
C G
wall And a ne - on sign will point the way to our bath - room down the
cans And when you're feel - ing mach - o you can crush - 'em like a
bar And a pay phone in the hall - way when your friends can't find their
1,2 3 D
hall She said "Just Gon - na Hire A
man" She said "We'll "You'll get friend - ly
car" She said I'm stead of a fami - ly
G D
Wi - no To Dec - o - rate Our Home So you feel more at ease here and
ser - vice and for add - ed at - mos - phere I'll slip on some - thing sex - y and
quar - rel we'll have a bar - room brawl when the Hamm's bear says it's clos - in' time you
A D
you won't need to roam we'll take out the din - ing room ta - ble put a
cut it clear to here then you can slap my bot - tom ev - 'ry
would'nt have far to crawl and when you run out of mon - ey then

G
D
bar a - long that wall__ and a ne - on sign will point the way__ to our bath -
time you tell a joke__ just as long as you keep tip - pin well__ I'll laugh__
you'll have me to thank__ you can sleep it off next morn - ing, ___ while I'm put -
A
D
1,2
3
E
room down the hall___ she said
__ un - til__ you're broke" she said in -
- tin' it in__ the bank" she said__ I'm__ Gon - na Hire A
A
E
Wi - no To Dec - o - rate__ Our Home__ So you'll feel more at ease here__ and
B
E
you won't need__ to roam__ Then when you and your friends get off___ from work and you'll__
A
E
have a pow-er-ful thirst___ Well there won't be an - y rea - son why__ you can't__

B
E
F♯
stop off here first
She said I'm
Gon - na Hire A
B
Wi - no To Dec - o - rate Our Home
So you'll feel more at
F♯
C♯
F♯
ease here and you won't need to roam
We'll take out the din - ing room
B
ta - ble put a bar a-long that wall
And a ne-on sign will
F♯
C♯
F♯
Repeat and Fade
point the way to our bath - room down the hall
She said I'm

I'M NO STRANGER TO THE RAIN

Words and Music by SONNY CURTIS
and RON HELLARD

C
I've fought with the dev - il, got
E♭
down on his lev - el. But I ne - ver gave in so he gave up on
B♭
C
me.
F
I'm no strang - er to the
rain.
B♭
I can spot bad weath - er, and I'm

F
good at find - ing shel - ter in a down - pour.
C
I've been sac - ri - ficed by broth - ers,
E♭
B♭
cru - ci - fied by lov - ers, but through it all I with - stood the
C
F
pain. I'm no strang - er to the rain. When I

B♭
F
get that fog - gy, feel - ing, what I'm a feel - ing now, If
(D.S.) Instrumental
B♭
F
I don't keep my head I may drown. But it's
Dm
Am
hard to keep be - liev - in' If I'll e - ven come out e - ven, while the
B♭
Gm
E♭
rain beats a hole in the ground, and to - night it's real - ly com - in'

C
To Coda
F
down.
I'm no strang-er to the rain,
But there'll
B♭
al - ways be to - mor - row and I'll
B♭
beg steal or bor - row a lit - tle
F
sun - shine.
C
I'll put this cloud be - hind me, that's
E♭
how the man de - signed me,
B♭
to ride the wind and dance in a hur - ri - cane.

C
Dm
I'm no strang - er to the rain, Oh
G7
B♭
C7
F
D.S. al Coda
no. I'm no strang - er to the rain.
CODA
F
B♭
I'm no strang - er to the rain. I'm a friend of thun - der, friend
F
is it a - ny won - der light - ning strikes me.

C
But I'll put this cloud_ be - hind me,___ that's
E♭
B♭
how the man de - signed me, to ride the wind and dance in a hur - ri - cane._
C
Dm
I'm no strang - er to___ the rain, Oh___
G7
B♭
C
F
no. I'm no strang - er to___ the rain.

IF HOLLYWOOD DON'T NEED YOU
(HONEY, I STILL DO)

F
To Coda
G
things back here they nev - er change at all.
all that I can think a - bout is you.
It
I
Am
F
C
snowed to - day, it's cold here for No - vem - ber
know this is what you've al - ways want - ed
but
but
Am
F
G
I hear the weath - er's warm out there.
I know now that all I want is you
Oh and
so
C
F
G
C
If you see Burt Rey - nolds would you shake his hand for me and
F
G
tell ol' Burt I've seen all his mov - ies.
Well I

C
F
G
C
F
hope you make the big time
I hope your dreams come true
But if Hol - ly - wood don't
G
Am
1
Am/G
C
need you
Hon-ey, I still
do.
2
G
F
G
Last
If
Hol - ly - wood don't
need you
Hon-ey, I still
C
D.S. al Coda
do.
CODA
G
C

ISLANDS IN THE STREAM

Moderately Slow Rock

Words and Music by BARRY GIBB, MAURICE GIBB and ROBIN GIBB

you do some-thing to me that I can't ex - plain Hold me clo - ser and I
that won't hap - pen to us and we got no doubt, too deep in love and we got
C7
F
feel no pain ev - 'ry beat of my heart we got some-thing go - in on
no way out and the mes-sage is clear, this could be the year for the
C
F
C
Fmaj7
real thing. Ten - der love is blind, It re - quires
No more will you cry. Ba - by I
Fm(+7)
a ded - i - ca - tion. All this love we feel needs no con - ver - sa - tion, we
will hurt you ne - ver. We start and end as one in love for ev - er, we can

C
ride it to - ge - ther ah - ah makin' love with each oth - er ah -
G7 C F
ah Is - lands in the stream that is what we are, no one in be -
Dm7 C
tween, How can we be wrong, sail a - way with me to an - oth - er
F C
world; and we re - ly on each oth - er ah - ah from one lo -

Dm7
1 C
- ver to a - no - ther ah - ah
2 C
F
Ab
ah
C
F C
F
Ab
C
G7
Is - lands in the

C
F
Dm7
stream, that is what we are no-one in be - tween, how can we be
C
F
wrong sail a - way with me to an - oth - er world and we re -
C
Dm7
- ly on each oth - er ha - hah from one lo - ver to a - noth - er ha -
C
G7
Repeat and Fade
hah Is - lands in the

LIFE TURNED HER THAT WAY

Words and Music by
HARLAN HOWARD

A
sid - er all she's gone through. Don't be
quick to con - demn her for
D
A
things she might say. Just re - mem - ber life
E
A
turned her that way. She's been

D
walked on__ and stepped on__ so man - y
A
times,__ and I hate to ad - mit it__ but the
E
last__ foot - print's__ mine.__
A
She was cry - in' when I

met her, she cries hard - er to -
D
A
E
day. So don't blame her life turned her that
1
A
way.
E
A
She's been

2
D
E
D/F♯
E/G♯
A
way.
So don't blame her life
E
A
turned her that way.
D/E
A

A LITTLE GOOD NEWS

Words and Music by TOMMY ROCCO, RORY BOURKE and CHARLIE BLACK
Slow 4
mf
C
F
F/G
C
mp
I rolled out this morn-ing the kids had the morn-ing news show on;
Bry-ant Gum-bel was talk-in' 'bout the fight-ing in
Am
F
Leb - a - non;
Some sen - a - tor was squawk-ing 'bout the bad e - con -
C
Am
Fmaj7
G7
- o - my.
It's gon-na get worse you see,
we need a change in pol - i - cy.

C
F
F/G
There's a lo - cal pa - per rolled up in a rub-ber band;
I'll come home this eve - nin' I'll bet that the news will be the same;
C
Am
One more sad sto-ry's one more than I can stand;
Some - bod - y takes a hos - tage, some-bod - y steals a plane;
F
C
Just once how I'd like to see the head - line say
"Not much to
How I wan-na hear the an-chor man talk a-bout a coun - ty fair
and how we cleaned
Am
Fmaj7
F/G
C CHORUS
print to-day, can't find noth - in' bad to say
be-cause
1. No-bod-y robbed a li-quor store on the
up the air, how ev-ery-bod-y learned to care,
Oh, tell me
2. No-bod-y was as-sas-si-nat-ed in the
f

F6
G9
C
low - er part of town,
whole third world to - day.
No - bod - y O. - D.'ed, no - bod-y burned a
And in the streets of Ire - land all the child - ren had
F6
G9
C
sin - gle build - ing down,
to do was play.
No - bod - y fired a shot in an - ger no -
And ev - ery - bod - y loves ev - ery - bod - y in the
F
Dm7
C
G7
- bod - y had to die in vain."
good old U. S. A.
We sure could use a lit - tle good news to -
D.S. and Fade
(Chorus 1)
1
C
F6
G7
C
F6
G7
day.
2
C
F
G
day.
mf

LOOKIN' FOR LOVE

Words and Music by WANDA MALLETTE,
PATTI RYAN and BOB MORRISON

D
game, hop - in' to win;
- ed or where it might end;
G
D
A
A/G
and tell - in' those sweet lies and los - in' a - gain.
I turned to a stran - ger just like a friend.
A/F#
A/E
D
I was look - in' for love in all the wrong plac - es,
I was look - in' for love in all the wrong plac - es,
look - in' for love in all the wrong plac - es,
F#m
G
look - in' for love in too man - y fac - es, search-in' their eyes and
look - in' for love in too man - y fac - es, search-in' their eyes and
look - in' for love in too man - y fac - es, search-in' their eyes and

Em
F♯m
G
A
look - in' for trac - es of what I'm dream - in' of.
look - in' for trac - es of what I'm dream - in' of.
look - in' for trac - es of what I'm dream - in' of.
D
F♯m
Hop - in' to find a friend and a lov - er; I'll bless the day
Hop - in' to find a friend and a lov - er; I'll bless the day
Now that I've found a friend and a lov - er; I bless the day
To Coda
G
Em
A
I dis - cov - er an - oth - er heart look - in' for love.
I dis - cov - er an - oth - er heart look - in' for love.
I dis - cov - ered
1
D
2
D

G
Then you came a - knock - in' at my heart's door; you're
Em
F♯m
G
A
ev - 'ry - thing I've been look - in' for.
D.S. al Coda
No more
CODA
you, oh
Em
A
D
you; look - in' for love in all the wrong plac - es;

F♯m
G
in too many - y fac - es, search - in' their eyes and
Em
F♯m
G
A
look - in' for trac - es of what I'm dream - in' of.
D
F♯m
Now that I've found a friend and a lov - er; I bless the day
G
Em
A
Repeat and Fade
I dis - cov - ered you, oh you; look - in' for love

MY BABY'S GOT GOOD TIMING

Moderate, bouncy country
By BOB McDILL
and DAN SEALS
G C G C/D G Em D
mf
I was lost time and all a - lone,
I'm feel - ing down,
when the world is qui - et,
an emp - ty heart with - out a home.
when the world clos - es in some - how;
and she's ly - ing here by my side;
Just at the time when I
just at the mo - ment when I
when it's her sweet love
need - ed a friend,
need her most,
I need,
she came a - long and she took me in. And ev'-ry
she comes to me and she
that's the mo - ment when she
1

2,3
D
G
Am/E
Em
C
G
holds me close.
comes to me.
My ba - by's got good tim - ing;
don't know how, but she reads
D
G
C
G
D
G
To Coda
my mind. And there's just one way to de - scribe it,
my ba - by's got good tim - ing.
C/D
G
D.S. al Coda
In the night
CODA
G
C/D
G
When she
Bm
C
D/F♯ G
D/F♯ G
Bm
loves me, she al - ways loves me right on time.
When she holds me she's oh,

C
Am7
D
G
so close I can feel her heart beat with mine.
C
G
D
G
Am/E
Em
C
G
My ba - by's got good tim - ing;
D
G
C
don't know how, but she reads my mind. And there's just one way to de - scribe it,
G
1 D
G
2 D
G
C/D
Gsus2
G
my ba - by's got good tim - ing. good tim - ing.

MY HEROES HAVE ALWAYS BEEN COWBOYS

Words and Music by
SHARON VAUGHN

Moderately slow
mf
F
Bb
I grew up a dreaming of being a cowboy, and loving the cowboy ways.
Cowboys are special with their own brand of mis'ry from being alone too long.
Pursuing the life of my high ridin' heroes, I burned up my childhood days.
You could die from the cold in the arms of a nightmare, knowing well that your best days are gone.
G7
C7

F
I learned all the rules of a mod-ern day drift-er, don't you
Pick-in' up hook-ers in-stead of my pen I let the
Bb
F
Bb
hold on to noth-in' too long.
words of my youth fade a-way.
Just take what you
Old worn out
F
Bb
F/C
C7
need from the la-dies then leave them with the words of a sad coun-try
sad-dles and old worn out mem-'ries with no one and no place to
F
Bb
F
song.
stay.
My he-roes have al-ways been cow-boys,

G7
C7
B♭
and they still are, it seems.
Sad - ly in
F
B♭
F
C7
To Coda
search of and one step in back of them - selves and their slow mov - in'
1. F
2. F
D.S. al Coda
dreams.
dreams.
CODA
B♭
F
B♭
F
dreams.

NOBODY IN HIS RIGHT MIND WOULD'VE LEFT HER

Words and Music by
DEAN DILLON

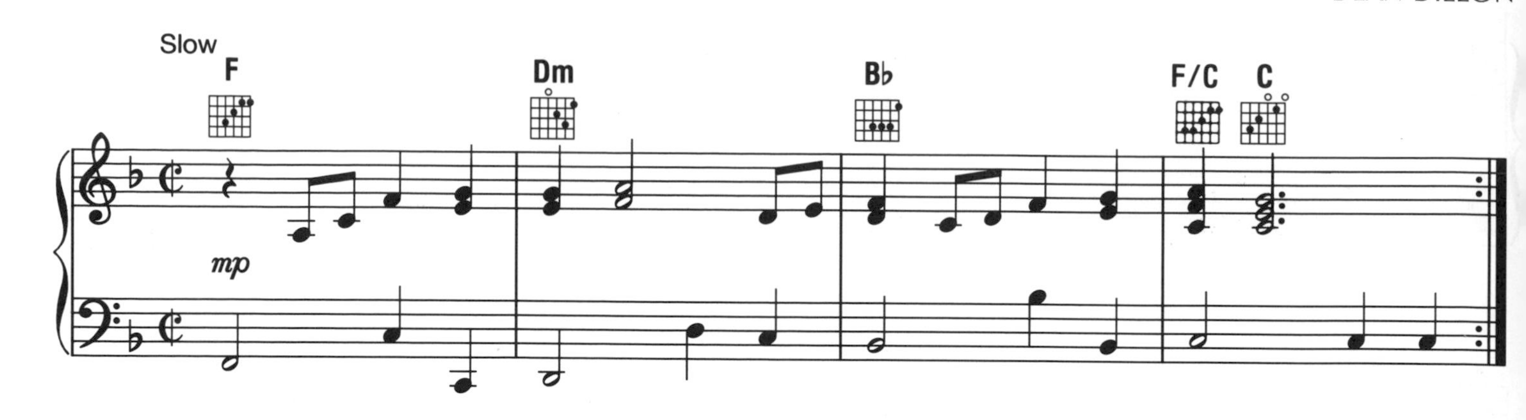

F
C
F
me
now.
She cried when I
Each night finds me
C
Dm
F/C
left her, now I cry to for - get her. Oh, how fool -
dream - in', each day I spend think - in' how much
B♭
C
- ish I was to ev - er want to leave.
I wish she was still a - round.
F
Dm
'Cause no - bod - y in his right mind would - 've
mf

B♭maj7
F
left her.
I had to be cra -
Dm
B♭maj7
C
- zy to say goodbye.
F
Dm
B♭maj7
No - bod - y in his right mind would - 've left her.
C
E - ven my heart was smart e - nough to stay be - hind.

F
Dm
1
B♭
F/C
C
C9
mp
2
B♭
C
Gm7
E - ven my heart was smart e - nough
C
F
Dm
to stay be - hind.
B♭
F/C
C
F
rit.

ON THE OTHER HAND

Words and Music by DON SCHLITZ
and PAUL OVERSTREET

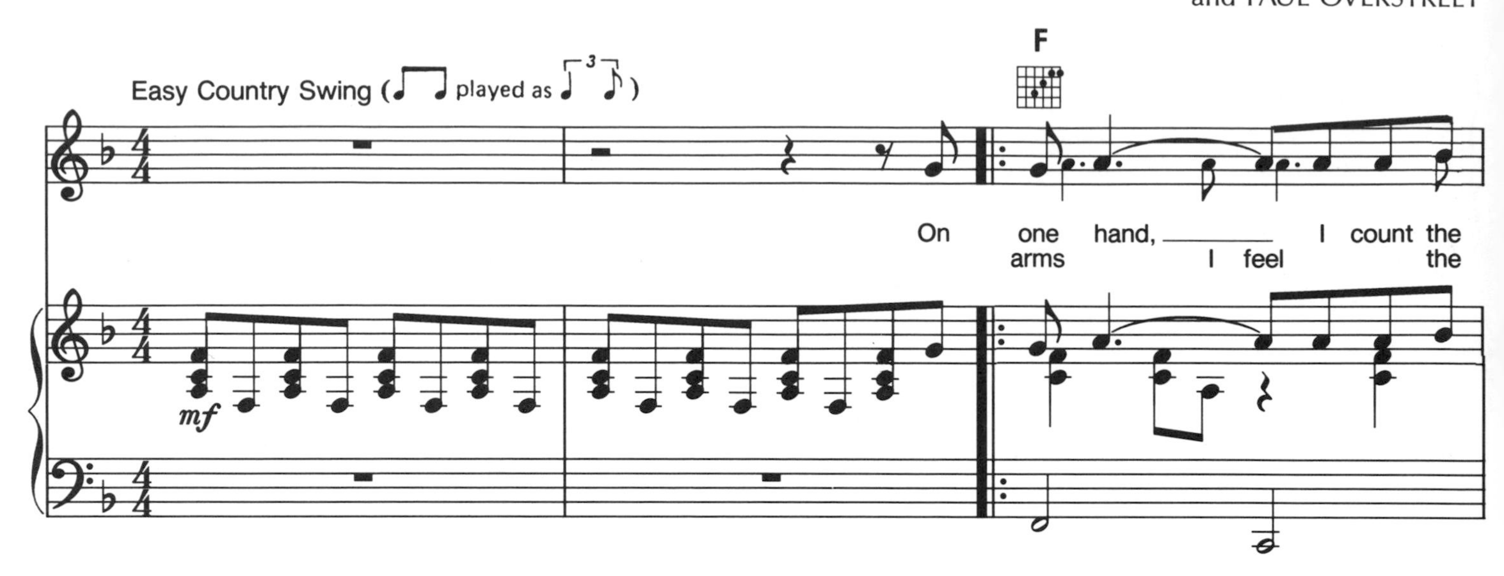

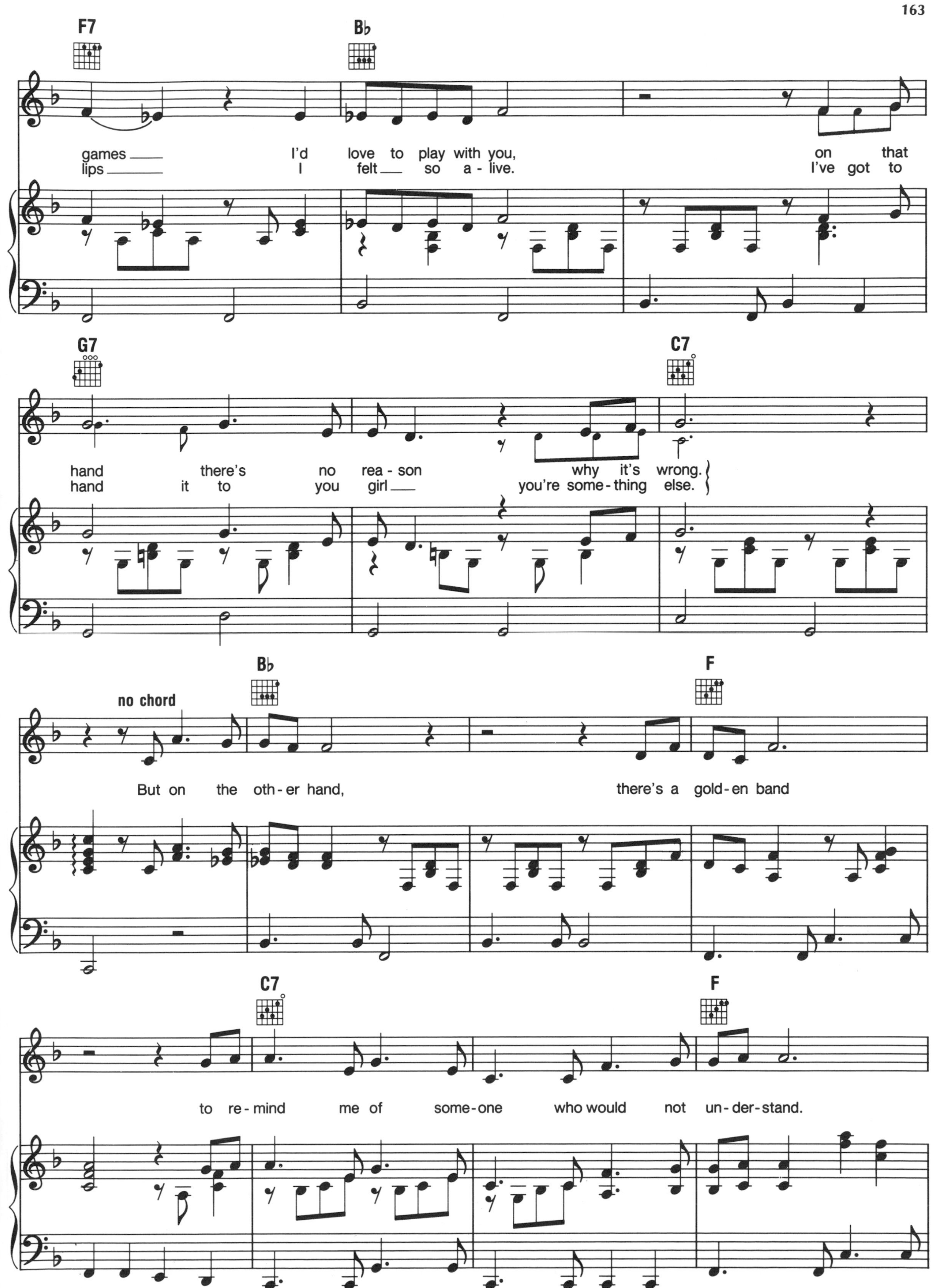
F7
Bb
games I'd love to play with you, on that
lips I felt so a-live. I've got to
G7
C7
hand there's no rea-son why it's wrong.
hand it to you girl you're some-thing else.
no chord
Bb
F
But on the oth-er hand, there's a gold-en band
C7
F
to re-mind me of some-one who would not un-der-stand.

B♭
F
On one hand I could stay and be your lov-ing man,
C7
F
but the rea - son I must go is on the oth-er hand.
3
1
2
In your
Yeah, the
3
3
C7
F
rea - son I must go is on the oth-er hand.
3
8va bassa

ROLL ON MISSISSIPPI

Words and Music by KYE FLEMING
and DENNIS MORGAN
Moderately
F
Am/E
Dm
mf
B♭
F
F
Walk - ing a - long,
Cool riv - er breeze
When the world's spin - ning 'round
Am/E
Dm7
whis - tling a song,
like pep - per - mint leaves,
too fast for me
bare - foot and fan -
the taste of it takes
I need a place
B♭
F
- cy free.
me back.
to dream.
A big riv - er boat
Chew - ing on straw,
So I come to your banks.

Am/E
Dm7
passing us by, she's headed for New
torn overalls, cane pole and old
I sit in your shade and relive the mem-
B♭
F
C7
Orleans. There she goes,
straw hat. Muddy river,
-ories. Tom Sawyer
F
B♭/F
disappearing around the bend.
just like a long lost friend.
and Huckleberry Finn.
F
C7
Roll on, Missis-sippi.

1
F
B♭/F
You make me feel like a child a - gain.
F
B♭/F
2-3
F
B♭
a - gain.
Roll on, Mis - sis -
F
B♭
F
B♭/C
sip - pi,
big riv - er roll.
F
C/E
Dm
You're the child - hood dream

Am
Gm7
C7
I grew up on.
Roll on, Mis - sis -
B♭
C
Dm
sip - pi,
car - ry me home.
B♭
Gm
Dm
Now I can see I've been a - way too long.
C7
B♭/C
F
Roll on,
Mis - sis -

B♭/F
To Coda
F
B♭/F
D.S. al Coda
sip - pi, roll on.
CODA
F
B♭/F
on.
Mis - sis -
F
B♭/F
F
sip - pi, roll on.
Whistle
B♭/F
F
B♭/F
Repeat and Fade

SET 'EM UP JOE

Moderately (♩♩ played as ♩ ♪ triplet)
Words and Music by DEAN DILLON, BUDDY CANNON, HANK COCHRAN and VERN GOSDIN
D
G
D
G
D
They got a
All my
G
D
vin - tage Vic - tro - la nine - teen fif - ty - one
ne - on neigh - bors they like what I play
3
full of my fav - 'rite re - cords that I
'cause they've heard it ev - 'ry night since you

G
D
grew up on.
walked a - way.
They got old
Ev - 'ry
Hank and Lef - ty and their B - twen - ty - four.
day they re - place old B - twen - ty - four 'cause ev - 'ry
set 'em up, Joe, and play "Walk - in' the Floor."
night I run a nee - dle through "Walk - in' the Floor." Ev - 'ry
Set 'em up, Joe, and play "Walk - in' the Floor."
night I run a nee - dle through "Walk - in' the Floor."

D G A

I'm gon - na spend the night like ev - 'ry

D A7

night be - fore

{play - in' E. T. and I'll}
{play - in' E. T. I'm gon - na}

D G A D

play him some more. I got - ta have a shot of them old trou - ba -

G
D
G
"Walk - in' the Floor."
Set 'em up, Joe, and play "Walk - in' the Floor."
D
D
I said set
'em up, Joe, and play "Walk - in' the Floor."
G
D
Set 'em up, Joe, and play "Walk - in' the Floor."
G
D

(SMOOTH AS) TENNESSEE WHISKEY

Words and Music by DEAN DILLON
and LINDA HARGROVE

F
Bb
I used to spend my nights out in a

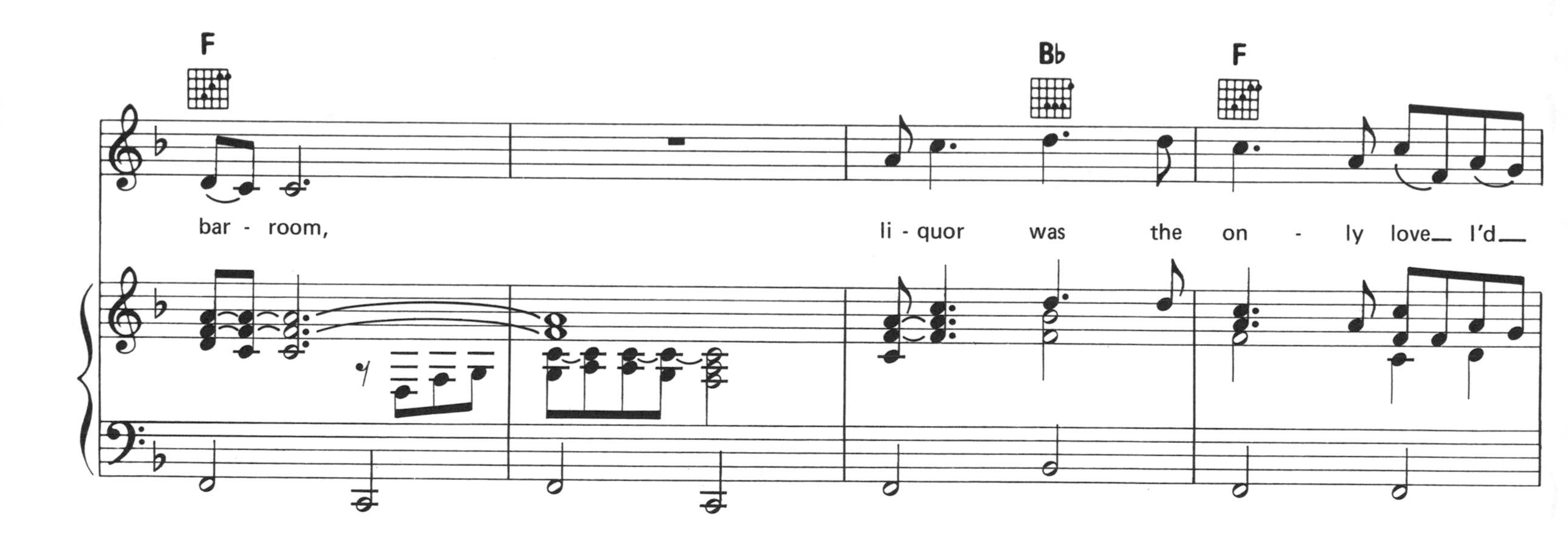
F
Bb
F
bar - room,
li - quor was the on - ly love I'd

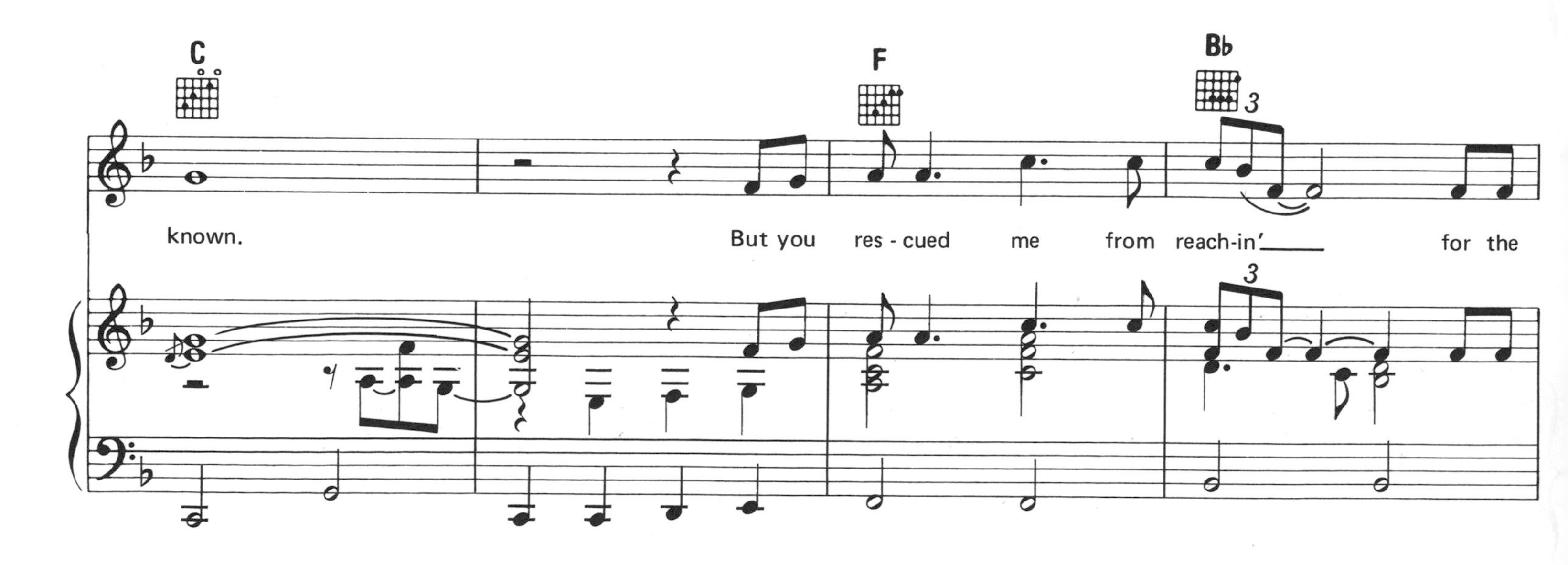
C
F
Bb
3
known.
But you res - cued me from reach-in' for the
3

F
B♭
bot - tom,
and you brought me back from
F/C
C
F
B♭
C
F
be - ing too far gone.
You're as smooth
B♭
F
as Tenn - es - see whis - key.
You're as sweet
C
F
as straw - ber - ry wine.
You're as warm

F7
Bb
F
as a glass of bran - dy, and I stay stoned on your
C7
F
Bb
F
love all the time.
C7
F
D7
G
I looked for love in
C
G
C
all the same old pla - ces, found the bot - tom of the

G D G
bot-tle al-ways dry. But when you poured out your
C G
heart I didn't waste it, 'cause there's
C G/D D7 G C D
noth-ing like your love to get me high. You're as
G C G
smooth as Tenn-es-see whis-key. You're as

D
sweet as straw - ber - ry - wine. You're as
G
G7
C
warm as a glass of bran - dy, and I stay
G
D
G
C
stoned on your love all the time. I stay
G/D
D7
C
G
stoned on your love all the time.

SWINGIN'

Words and Music by JOHN DAVID ANDERSON
and LIONEL A. DELMORE

With a strong beat
f
E7
mf
1. There's a lit-tle girl in our neigh-bor-hood. Her
2.3. (See additional lyrics)
name is Char-lotte John-son, and she's real-ly look-ing good. I had to go and see her, so I
called her on the phone. I walked o-ver to her house, and this was go-in' on: 2. Her

2,3
CHORUS
A7
love down to my toes. And we was swing-in', (swing-in';) yes, we was
E7
B7
swing-in'. (swing-in'.) Lit-tle Char-lotte, she's as pret-ty as the
Bb7
A7
an-gels when they sing. I can't be-lieve I'm out here on her front porch in the swing, just a
E7
To Coda
D.S. (3rd ending) al Coda
swing-in'. (Swing-in'.) 3. Now
CODA
Lit-tle

Verse 2.
Her brother was on the sofa
Eatin' chocolate pie.
Her mama was in the kitchen
Cuttin' chicken up to fry.
Her daddy was in the backyard
Rollin' up a garden hose.
I was on the porch with Charlotte
Feelin' love down to my toes,
And we was swingin'. *(To Chorus:)*

Verse 3.
Now Charlotte, she's a darlin';
She's the apple of my eye.
When I'm on the swing with her
It makes me almost high.
And Charlotte is my lover.
And she has been since the spring.
I just can't believe it started
On her front porch in the swing. *(To Chorus:)*

SOMEBODY SHOULD LEAVE

Words and Music by HARLAN HOWARD and CHICK RAINS

Moderate Country Ballad
D
A/D
G/D
D
A/D
mf
G/D
D
A/D
G
D
A/D
G
D
D7
G
D/F♯
It sure gets qui - et when the kids go to
You say good night and turn and face the
Em7
A7
bed.
wall.
We sit here in the si - lence, put - ting
We lie here in the dark - ness, and the

G
A
D
off what must be___ said.
tears start to___ fall.
I read a book, you
If it was on - ly
D7
G
D/F♯
Em
watch T. V.___
you and me___
as our love__ dies___ qui - et - ly.___
good-bye might__ come more___ eas - i - ly.___
G
A
D
I'm so sad__ I don't know__ what__ I've just__ read.
But what a - bout__ those__ ba - bies__down the___ hall.
G
A
D
G
D
Some-bod-y should leave,___ but which one should it be?

Bm
Em7
You need the kids, and they need me.
A
D
D7
G
Some-bod-y should leave, but we hate to give in.
A7
We keep hop-in' some-how we might need each oth-er a-gain.
1 D
A/D
G
D
A/D

G
2 D
G A
Some-bod - y should leave,
D
D7
G
but we hate to give in.
A7
D
A/D
Spoken: We just keep hopin' we might need each other again.
G
D
A/D
G
D

TIMBER I'M FALLING IN LOVE

Words and Music by
KOSTAS

D
G
A
Tim - ber, I'm fall - in' in
Tim - ber, I'm fall - in' in
D
G
D
A
To Coda
D
love.
love.
It start - ed slow,
Instrumental
G
D
it's com - in' fast. I got a feel - ing,
A
D
it's gon - na last. Tim - ber, I'm

G
A
D
G
D
fall - ing in love.
G
A
You're so pret - ty, you look so sweet.
You're so pret - ty, you look so sweet.
D
Your love's sweep - in' me off of my feet. You're
G
C
the on - ly one, I'm dream - in' of. I

F
B♭
can't be - lieve that I'm fall - ing in
A
1
2
D.S. al Coda
love.
CODA
D
G
A
Tim - ber, I'm fall - ing in
D
G
1 D
A
2 D
A
D
love.

TO ALL THE GIRLS I'VE LOVED BEFORE

Moderately slow, with expression
Lyric by HAL DAVID
Music by ALBERT HAMMOND
G
D/G
C/G
G
mf
G
To all the girls I've loved be - fore, who trav - eled in and
once car - essed, and may I say I've
shared my life, who now are some - one
Am7
Am7/D
D7
out my door; I'm glad they came a - long, I ded - i - cate this
held the best; for help - ing me to grow, I owe a lot, I
els - e's wife; I'm glad they came a - long, I ded - i - cate this

Am7/D
D7
To Coda
G
C/G
G
song to all the girls I've loved be - fore.
know, to all the girls I've loved be - fore.
song to all the girls I've
To all the girls I
G
C/G
G
The winds of change are al - ways blow - ing
and ev - 'ry time I tried to
3
Am7
Am7/D
D7
stay.
The winds of change con - tin - ued blow - ing,
Am7/D
D7
G
C/G
G
D.S. al Coda
and they just car - ried me a - way.
To all the girls who

CODA
C/G
G
E♭7sus
A♭
loved be - fore.
1. To all the girls who
cared for me;
(2,3.) loved be - fore;
B♭m7
who filled my nights with ec - sta - sy;
who trav - eled in and out our door;
they live with - in my
we're glad they came a -
B♭m7/E♭
E♭7
B♭m7/E♭
E♭7
heart; I'll al - ways be a part of all the girls I've loved be - fore.
long; we ded - i - cate this song to all the girls we've
1
A♭
D♭/A♭
A♭
To next strain
The winds of change are al - ways
2
D♭/A♭
A♭
D♭/A♭
A♭
loved be - fore.
2. To all the girls we've

3
Fb
Gb
Ab
Fine
loved
be - fore.
8va
Db/Ab
Ab
Bbm7
blow - ing
3
and ev 'ry time I tried to stay,
Bbm7/Eb
Eb7
Bbm7/Eb
Eb7
The winds of change con - tin - ued blow - ing,
and they just car - ried me a -
Fb
Ab
way.
3. To all the girls we've

TENNESSEE FLAT TOP BOX

Words and Music by
JOHNNY CASH
Bright Country Two-Beat
B♭
mf
E♭
3-
B♭
In a
Well, he
Then
lit - tle cab - a - ret___ in a South Tex - as
could - n't ride or wran - gle and he nev - er cared to
one day he was gone___ and no - one ev - er

F7
bor - der - town, sat a boy and his gui - tar,
make a dime, But give him his gui - tar,
saw him 'round. He van - ished like the breeze.

B♭
and the peo - ple came from all a - round. And
and he'd be hap - py all the time. And
They for - got him in the lit - tle town, But

all the girls from there to
all the girls from nine to
all the girls still dreamed a -

F
Aus - tin were slip-ping a - way from
nine - ty were snap-ping fin - gers,
bout him and hung a - round the

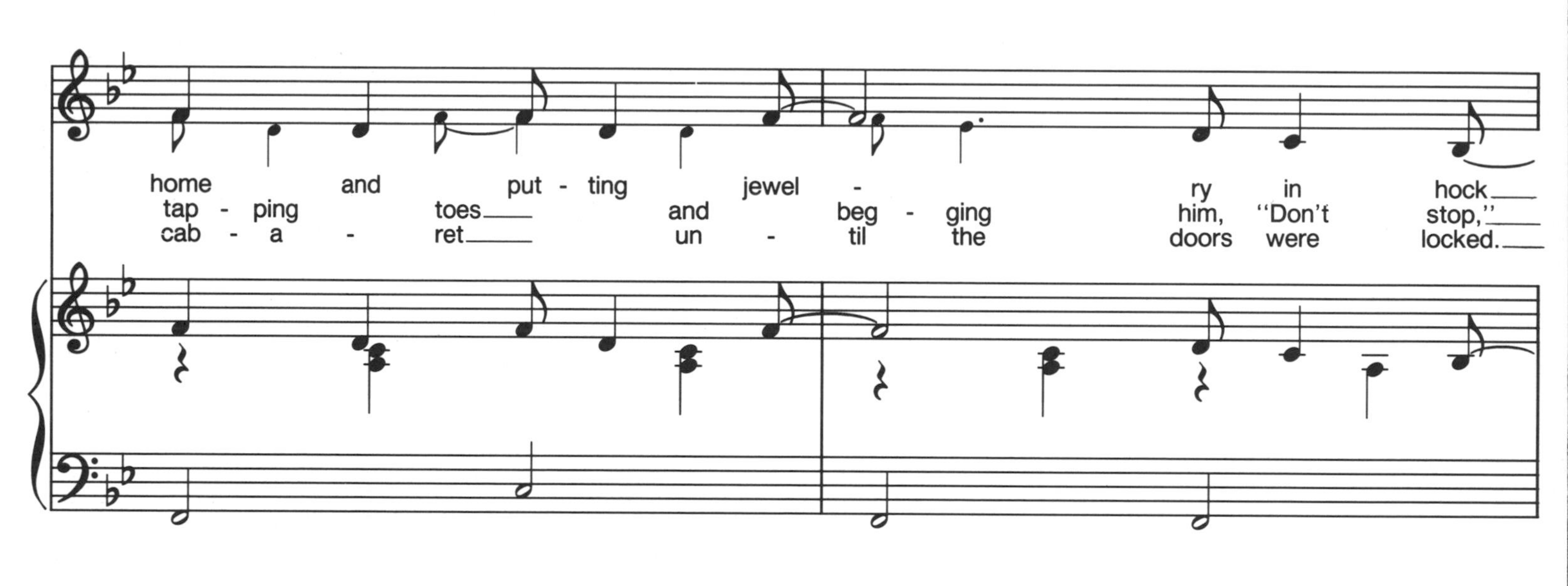
home and put - ting jewel - ry in hock
tap - ping toes and beg - ging him, "Don't stop,"
cab - a - ret un - til the doors were locked.

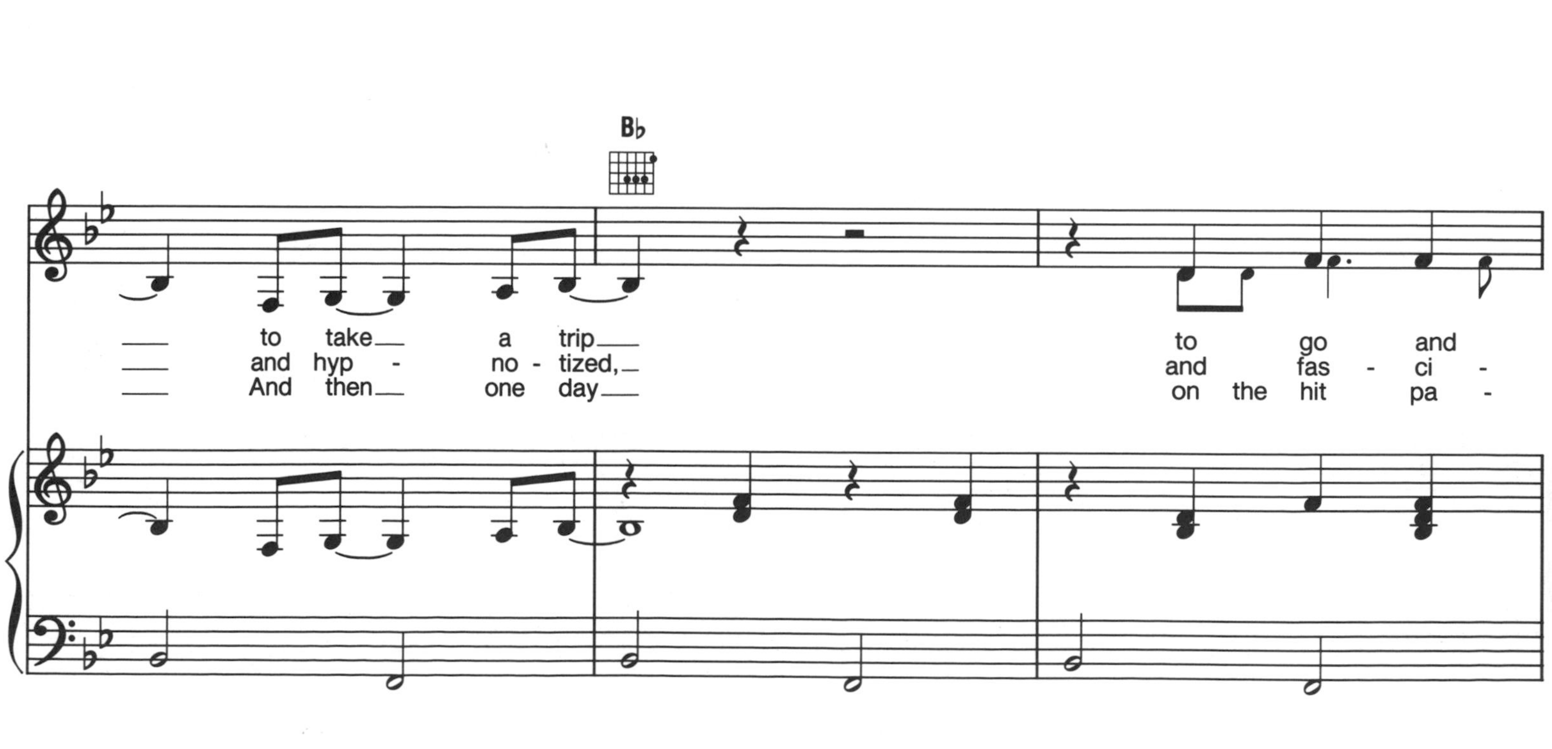
B♭
to take a trip to go and
and hyp - no - tized, and fas - ci -
And then one day on the hit pa -

F
lis - ten
na - ted
rade
to the
by the
was a
lit - tle dark - haired
Bb
boy who played the Ten - nes - see flat top box. And he would
Eb
play.
Bb

E♭
3-
B♭
1,2
E♭
3-
3
E♭
3-
B♭
Repeat and Fade

WANDERING EYES

Words and Music by
JAMIE O'HARA

D
G
heart al - ways stays here at home.
Well, I
Instrumental
saw you look at me when you saw me look at her. And
D
there was no de - ny - ing what went through your mind. You were
G
C
G
filled with jeal - ous - y. Oh, but there's no need to be. I'm just

D
1
G
2
G
look-ing, girl, not look-ing_ to find._
I got _
I got
C
G
wan - der - ing eyes._ Yes, it's true_ I love the la - dies. I
D
can't de-ny_ the feel - ing the Good Lord put down in my bones._ I got
G
C
G
wan - der - ing eyes._ Oh, but don't_ you wor - ry, ba - by. My

D
G
A♭
heart al-ways stays here at home.
You should know by now, dar-ling, when I took those vows
I meant ev-'ry word that preach-er
E♭
A♭
D♭
A♭
told me to say. It seems so un-nat-u-ral when I see a pret-ty girl to
E♭7
A♭
turn my head and look the oth - er way. I got

D♭
A♭
wan - der - ing eyes. Yes, it's true I love the la - dies. I
E♭
can't de - ny the feel - ing the Good Lord put down in my bones. I got
A♭
D♭
A♭
wan - der - ing eyes. Oh, but don't you wor - ry, ba - by. My
E♭
A♭
Repeat and Fade
heart al - ways stays here at home. I got

THE WAY I AM

Words and Music by
SONNY THROCKMORTON

G
D7
1
G
dream and keep on be - ing the way I am. Wish I en -
2
G
C
am. The way I am don't fit my
G
D7
G
shack - les, the way I am, re - al - i - ty. I can al - most
C
G
D7
see that bob - ber danc - ing, but I just dream and keep on be - in' the way I

G
C
E7/B
Am
G/D
D7
am.
G
G
D7
The way I am. I just dream, keep on be - in' the way I
G
C
G
am.
C
G6

WHAT'S FOREVER FOR

Words and Music by
RAFE VANHOY

D7sus
G
Am7
D7sus
- zy, but I can't un - der - stand why;
- ple, try - ing their best to sur - vive; when
G
Am7
G/B
C
all these lov - ers keep hurt - ing each oth - er, when
right there in their hands is a dy - ing ro - mance, and they're not
G/D
D7sus
good love is so hard to come by.
e - ven trying to keep it a - live.
G
Em
Am7
D7sus
So what's the glo - ry in liv - ing? Does - n't
mf
8va-

G
Em
Am7
D7sus
an - y - bod - y ev - er stay___ to - geth - er an - y - more?___
G
Am7
G/B
C
G/D
D7sus
To Coda
And if love__ nev - er lasts for - ev - er, tell me: What's for - ev - er for?_
1
G
Am7
Bm
Am7
mp
2
G
D7sus
D.S. al Coda
CODA
G
Am7
G/B
C
D7sus
G
decresc.
rit.

WHO'S CHEATIN' WHO

Words and Music by
JERRY HAYES

C
G
C
some - thing that you don't un - der - stand. Still you won - der
How could I be so blind? But still you won - der
long as they keep out of sight. But still you won - der
F
who's cheat - in' who and who's be - ing true,
C
G
B♭
who don't e - ven care an - y - more? It makes you won - der
C
F7
who's do - in' right to some - one to - night and

C
G
To Coda
1 C
whose car is parked next door? I
2 C
door? Gui - tar.
G
C
F
C
G
C
D.S. al Coda
A

CODA
C
door. Still you won-der who's cheat - in' who and
F
who's be - ing true,
C
who don't e - ven care an - y -
G
more?
B♭
It makes you won-der
C
who's do - in' right to
F7
some-one to - night and
C
whose car
G
is parked next
C
door?
Repeat and Fade
But still you won-der

WHY NOT ME

Medium Country

Words and Music by HARLAN HOWARD, SONNY THROCKMORTON and BRENT MAHER

old home town your Ken - tuck - y girl's been a - wait - ing pa - tient -
world was round. It's time that you learned how good set - tl - ing down could
Fmaj9
C
G
ly. Why not me?
be. Why not me?
Why not me
D
D7
C
on a rain - y day? Why not me to love your cares a - way? Why not me?
G
D
Why not me when the nights get cold?

D7
C
G
Why not me when you're grow - ing old?
Why not me?
1
2
D.S. al Coda
(verse 1)
You've been
You've been
CODA
C
G
Why not me?
Why not me?
Dsus
G
Ba-by, why not me?

YOU DON'T KNOW ME

Words and Music by
CINDY WALKER and EDDY ARNOLD
Moderately Slow
G7+5
C
You give your hand to me and then you
mp
mf
C7
F
F#dim
say hel-lo, I can hard-ly speak, my heart is beat-ing so, And an-y
C
A7
Dm7
G7
C
one could tell you think you know me well, but You Don't Know Me.
D7
G7
G7+5
C
C7
No, you don't know the one who dreams of you at night and longs to

F
F#dim
C
A7
kiss your lips and longs to hold you tight. To you I'm just a friend, that's all I've
Dm7
G7
C
F
C
C7
F
ev-er been, but You Don't Know Me. For I nev-er knew the
C
C#dim
Dm
G7
C
art of mak - ing love, though my heart ached with love for you.
Am
Em
D7
A-fraid and shy, I let my chance go by, the chance that you might love me

G7
Dm7
G7
G7+5
C
C7
too. You give your hand to me and then you say good-bye. I watch you
F
F♯dim
C
A7
walk a-way beside the luck-y guy. You'll nev-er nev-er know the one who
Dm7
G7
C
F
C
C7
C
F♯dim
loves you so; no, You Don't Know Me. For Know Me You'll nev-er
C
A7
Dm7
G7
C
G7sus
G7
C
nev-er know the one who loves you so; no, You Don't Know Me.
rit.

YOU'RE THE REASON GOD MADE OKLAHOMA

A
D
mem - ber is all that I do.
Los - in' you left a
G
D
A
D
pret - ty good cow - boy with noth - in' to hold on to.
G
Sun-down came and I drove to town and drank a drink or two.
Bridge
D
G
D
3
You're The Rea - son God Made Ok - la - ho - ma.
You're The Rea - son God Made

2. Here the city lights outshine the moon
I was just now thinking of you
Sometimes when the wind blows you can see the mountains
And all the way to Malibu
Everyone's a star here in L.A. County
You ought to see the things that they do.
All the cowboys down on the Sunset Strip
Wish they could be like you.
The Santa Monica Freeway
Sometimes makes a country girl blue

(BRIDGE)

3. I worked ten hours on a John Deere tractor,
Just thinkin of you all day. . . .
I've got a calico cat and a two
room flat, on a
street in West L.A.